Corpus Exploration of Lexis and Discourse in Translation

This edited volume reflects on the development of corpus translation studies as a rapidly growing, diversified field of translation studies. It examines the evolving identity of corpus translation from a marginal research tactic focusing on generating numeric corpus attributes to a powerful and increasingly sophisticated corpus analytical scheme and methodological paradigm that has significantly changed and continues to shape our understanding of the research and practical, social values of empirical translation studies.

Since its inception in the 1990s, corpus translation studies have permeated through almost every corner and branch of contemporary translation studies – from literary translation stylistics, through cognitive and neural translation, to more socially oriented translation studies, such as health care, environmental, and political and policy translation. Corpus methodological innovation has become a central research aim and priority in some of the most dynamic areas of translation studies. Methodological advancement has as its main aim a better, enhanced understanding on the part of translation studies scholars of the internal factors and external variables that may account for the prevalence of certain translation features (for example, corpus textual and linguistic patterns).

This edited collection presents the latest studies of corpus-based and corpus-driven specialised translation and will appeal to students and scholars of translation studies, in particular those interested in corpus translation.

Meng Ji is Associate Professor of Translation Studies at the School of Languages and Cultures, the University of Sydney, Australia.

Michael P. Oakes is Reader in the Research Institute for Information and Language Processing, University of Wolverhampton, United Kingdom.

Routledge Studies in Empirical Translation and Multilingual Communication
Series Editor: Meng Ji
The University of Sydney, Australia

Empirical Translation Studies (ETS) represents a rapidly growing field of research which came to the fore in the 1990s. From the early tentative use of computerised translation to the systematic investigation of large-scale translation corpora by using quantitative/statistical methods, ETS has made substantial progress in the development of solid empirical research methodologies which lie at the heart of the further development of the field. There is a growing volume of research pursued in ETS as corpus translation studies has become a core component of translation studies at the postgraduate and research levels. To offer an appropriate and much-needed outlet for high-quality research in ETS, this book series selects and publishes latest translation research from around the world, in which the innovative use of corpus materials and related methodologies is essential. An important shared feature of these titles is their original contribution made to the advancement of empirical methodologies in translation studies which includes, but is not limited, to the quantitative/statistical processing, modelling and interpretation of translation corpora.

Translating and Communicating Environmental Cultures
Edited by Meng Ji

Form, Meaning and Function in Collocation
A Corpus Study on Commercial Chinese-to-English Translation
Haoda Feng

Corpus Exploration of Lexis and Discourse in Translation
Edited by Meng Ji and Michael P. Oakes

For more information about this series, please visit www.routledge.com/Routledge-Studies-in-Empirical-Translation-and-Multilingual-Communication/book-series/RSET

Corpus Exploration of Lexis and Discourse in Translation

Edited by Meng Ji and Michael P. Oakes

LONDON AND NEW YORK

First published 2022
by Routledge
2 Park Square, Milton Park, Abingdon, Oxon OX14 4RN

and by Routledge
605 Third Avenue, New York, NY 10158

Routledge is an imprint of the Taylor & Francis Group, an Informa business

© 2022 selection and editorial matter, Meng Ji and Michael P. Oakes; individual chapters, the contributors

The right of Meng Ji and Michael P. Oakes to be identified as the authors of the editorial material, and of the authors for their individual chapters, has been asserted in accordance with sections 77 and 78 of the Copyright, Designs and Patents Act 1988.

All rights reserved. No part of this book may be reprinted or reproduced or utilised in any form or by any electronic, mechanical, or other means, now known or hereafter invented, including photocopying and recording, or in any information storage or retrieval system, without permission in writing from the publishers.

Trademark notice: Product or corporate names may be trademarks or registered trademarks and are used only for identification and explanation without intent to infringe.

British Library Cataloguing-in-Publication Data
A catalogue record for this book is available from the British Library

Library of Congress Cataloguing-in-Publication Data
A catalog record for this book has been requested

ISBN: 978-0-367-60961-0 (hbk)
ISBN: 978-0-367-60962-7 (pbk)
ISBN: 978-1-003-10269-4 (ebk)

DOI: 10.4324/9781003102694

Typeset in Times New Roman
by Apex CoVantage, LLC

Contents

List of Figures vii
List of Tables viii
List of Contributors ix
Introduction xiii

1 A corpus-based analysis of medical communication: euphemism as a communication strategy for context-specific responses 1
SONIA ASMAHÈNE HALIMI, RAZIEH AZARI, PIERRETTE BOUILLON, AND HERVÉ SPECHBACH

2 MDA analysis of translated and non-translated parliamentary discourse 26
MARÍA CALZADA-PÉREZ AND MARÍA DEL MAR SÁNCHEZ RAMOS

3 Corpus-based analysis of Russian translations of *Animal Farm* by George Orwell 56
MIKHAIL MIKHAILOV

4 Exploring semantic annotations to measure post-editing quality 83
FELIPE ALMEIDA COSTA, THIAGO CASTRO FERREIRA, ADRIANA SILVINA PAGANO, AND WAGNER MEIRA, JR.

5 **Analyzing multiword term formation as a means to facilitate translation** 105
MELANIA CABEZAS-GARCÍA

Index 123

Figures

2.1	Example of LSTO results	36
2.2	Biber's dimension 1	39
2.3	ECPC (original and translated) subcorpora's dimension 1	40
2.4	Biber's dimension 2	43
2.5	ECPC (original and translated) subcorpora's dimension 2	44
2.6	Biber's dimension 6	49
2.7	ECPC (original and translated) subcorpora's dimension 6	50
3.1	Distance measure visualisation (MDS)	70
4.1	Example of a single instance in the WebNLG corpus	87
4.2	Screenshot of free mode PE system developed for data collection	89
4.3	Screenshot of guided mode PE system developed for data collection	90
4.4	Screenshot of evaluation system developed for data collection	91
4.5	Post-editing quality distribution	93
5.1	Sample of the verb paraphrases for *power curve*	112

Tables

1.1	Selected sentences representing defined criteria	9
1.2	Communication strategies used by the doctors	11
1.3	Communication strategies used by the nonmedical translator	16
3.1	A fragment of a bitext with machine translation	64
3.2	*Animal Farm* and its translations	66
3.3	A fragment from the joint frequency table	69
3.4	A fragment of the keyword list from the translation by Struve & Kriger	72
3.5	Part of speech statistics in the keyword lists	73
4.1	Example of an RDF structure	86
4.2	Post-edited texts per category and triple set size	92
4.3	Linear regression output	95
4.4	Comics character category example	95
4.5	Food category example	96
4.6	Co-reference pronoun example	97
4.7	Example of low quality achieved after post-editing of a 5 triple-verbalization	98
4.8	Triple set for verbalization	98
4.9	Post-editing (PE) quality and machine translation (MT) confusion matrix	99
4.10	Post-edited text rated higher than its machine-translated counterpart	99
4.11	Post-edited text rated lower than its machine-translated counterpart	99
5.1	Example of CQL query to extract MWTs including a specific term (*generator*)	110
5.2	Assignment of semantic categories in *generator torque control*	111
5.3	Example of a CQL query to extract verb paraphrases	111
5.4	Example of CQL query to extract free paraphrases	112
5.5	Slots opened by the ENTITY>CREATION category	116

Contributors

Razieh Azari is a PhD student in translation studies at the Faculty of Translation and Interpreting and an MSc student in global health at the Institute of Global Health, University of Geneva, Switzerland. She has several publications focusing on lay-friendliness of health-related information, health communication, crowdsourcing translation, and culture.

Pierrette Bouillon has been Professor at the FTI ("Faculty of Translation and Interpreting"), University of Geneva, since 2007. She is currently Director of the Department of Translation Technology and Dean of the FTI. She has numerous publications in computational linguistics and natural language processing, particularly within lexical semantics (generative lexicon theory), speech-to-speech machine translation for limited domains, post-editing and more recently accessibility. She is now head of the new Swiss SNF Propicto project, "PRojection du langage Oral vers des unités PICTOgraphiques – PROPICTO".

Melania Cabezas-García holds degrees in translation and interpreting from the University Pablo de Olavide and the University of Granada, where she teaches courses in the bachelor's degree in translation and interpreting. She received her PhD in translation and interpreting from the University of Granada in 2019. In 2020, she was awarded the PhD Prize of the Iberian Association of Translation and Interpreting Studies (Asociación Ibérica de Estudios de Traducción e Interpretación), which recognizes the most outstanding PhD dissertation of the last two years (2019–2020). She is a member of the LexiCon research group, and her research interests are terminology, corpus linguistics, and specialized translation. She has published papers in international journals on linguistics, terminology, and specialized translation and serves on the scientific boards of international journals and conferences, such as LREC and the *International Journal of Lexicography*.

x Contributors

María Calzada-Pérez is Full Professor of Translation Studies at the Universitat Jaume I (Spain). Her research mainly focuses on corpus-based translation studies, institutional translation (especially translation at the European Parliament), translation pedagogy, ideology, and advertising. She is Principal Coordinator of the ECPC (European Comparable and Parallel Corpora of Parliamentary Speeches) research group. She has produced books and papers such as *Transitivity in Translating: The Interdependence of Texture and Context* (Peter Lang, 2007); "Five Turns of the Screw. A CADS analysis of the European Parliament" (*Journal of Language and Politics*, 2017); "Corpus-based methods for Comparative Translation and Interpreting Studies" (*Translation and Interpreting Studies*, 2017); "Researching the European Parliament with Corpus-Assisted Discourse Studies. From the micro- and macro-levels of text to the macro-context" (*Pragmatics* 29(3), 357–383); "A corpus-assisted SFL approach to individuation in the European Parliament: the case of Sánchez Presedo's original and translated repertoires" (*Meta. Translators' Journal*, 65(1), 142–167). She is also editor of volumes such as *Apropos of Ideology* (St. Jerome, 2003); *MonTI* 13 and *Meta. Translators' Journal*, 65(1).

Felipe Almeida Costa is a graduate student in computer science at Universidade Federal de Minas Gerais, Brazil, where he received his BSc in information systems. He is interested in computational linguistics, more specifically in human–machine cooperation for NLP tasks. Currently, he is writing his MSc dissertation on post-editing of machine-translation output.

Thiago Castro Ferreira is a postdoctoral research fellow at Universidade Federal de Minas Gerais, Brazil, and works at aiXplain as an Applied AI/ML Engineer. He holds a PhD in computational linguistics from the University of Tilburg, Netherlands, where he was also a postdoctoral fellow. He has conducted several research projects in the fields of natural language generation, question-answering, semantic web, and artificial intelligence and lectured several courses in computer science and computational linguistics.

Sonia Asmahène Halimi has been Professor at the Faculty of Translation and Interpreting (FTI), University of Geneva, since 2013. After long experience as professional translator in the United Nations agencies, she is presently head of the Arabic unit at the FTI. She teaches pragmatic translation and translation in legal and economic fields (English–Arabic, French–Arabic). She has various publications in legal translation, natural language processing with Arabic, health communication, and teaching translation. She is now head of the e-Ba program in Multilingual communication and member of the Centre of Legal and Institutional Translation Studies (Transius).

Wagner Meira, Jr. is Professor of Computer Science at Universidade Federal de Minas Gerais, Brazil, where he is currently the chair of the computer science department. He has an extensive publication list in top venues and is co-author of *Data Mining and Analysis* and *Data Mining and Machine Learning*, both published by Cambridge University. His research focuses on scalability and efficiency of large scale parallel and distributed systems, from massively parallel to Internet-based platforms, and on data mining algorithms, their parallelization, and application to areas such as information retrieval, bioinformatics, e-governance, and cybersecurity.

Mikhail Mikhailov is Professor of Translation Studies (Finnish and Russian) at the Tampere University, Finland. He is one of the authors of the book "Corpus Linguistics for Translation and Contrastive Studies" (Routledge 2016). He compiles multilingual corpora and develops web-based corpus software. His research covers corpus-based translation studies with a particular focus on parallel and comparable corpora, terminological studies, and translation technologies.

Adriana Silvina Pagano is Professor of Translation Studies at Universidade Federal de Minas Gerais, Brazil, where she advises doctoral theses in the Graduate Program in Linguistics and Applied Linguistics and conducts research at the Laboratory for Experimentation in Translation. She is interested in multilingual modeling of meaning and is currently engaged in multidisciplinary projects in the health care domain.

María del Mar Sánchez Ramos is Associate Professor in the Department of Modern Philology at the University of Alcalá (Madrid, Spain), where she teaches translation technology and specialised translation. She holds a PhD in Translation and Interpreting from the Universitat Jaume I (Castellón, Spain). Her research is mainly focused on corpus-based translation studies, public service translation and translation technology. Her publications have appeared in various books (e.g., Routledge, Springer, Cambridge University Press) and journals such as *Babel, Translation and Interpreting Studies* or *Lebende Sprachen*. She is also an active member of different research projects, such as "Original, translated and interpreted representations of the refugee cris(e)s: methodological triangulation within corpus-based discourse studies" (Universitat Jaume I, Castellón, Spain); and "Research and training in public service interpreting and translation" (Universidad de Alcalá, Madrid, Spain).

xii *Contributors*

Hervé Spechbach is medical doctor at the University Hospitals of Geneva since 2006 and head of outpatient emergency service since 2015. He has many publications in the field of informatics for health care. He is representing the University Hospitals of Geneva in the Swiss center for barrier-free communication and co-leads the babelDr project, an innovative and reliable medical phraselator, which received in 2018 an innovation award from University Hospitals of Geneva.

Introduction

This book contains five recent studies on corpus-based empirical translation studies. The title was chosen because two of them are concerned with lexis (multiword technical terms and words used in doctor–patient interaction), while the other three are concerned with discourse (dimensions of register in text, six translations of *Animal Farm*, and measuring machine translation quality). Specifically, the chapters are as follows:

Halimi and Bouillon present a corpus-based analysis of medical communication for context-specific responses. They were particularly interested in the translation of potentially embarrassing terms related to sexual health and bodily functions in doctor–patient conversations. The translations preferred by Persian doctors of a corpus of French medical questions were not always the same as those suggested by the BabelDr machine translation system, and so the doctors could influence future design of BabelDr's phrase lists. This chapter contains some interesting thoughts on the nature and purpose of euphemism.

María Calzada-Pérez and María del Mar Sánchez Ramos follow De Sutter and Lefer's (2020) new agenda for empirical translation studies, which follows the stages of Biber's (1988) multidimensional analysis (MDA). They compare corpora of both original and translated texts and determine the extent to which they can find Biber's original dimensions of text. Two of the stages of particular interest are (1) the identification and annotation of the 67 linguistic features originally found by Biber to distinguish registers of speech and text, using Nini's (2014, 2019) MAT,[1] and (2) the use of Brezina's Lancaster Stats Tool Online (LSTO),[2] which performs the graphical analysis of the linguistic features and their frequencies to produce plots showing which features are typical of which extremes of register and, simultaneously, which texts belonged to which registers. Clearest results were found for Biber's dimensions 1 (informational versus involved production), 2 (narrative versus non-narrative concerns) and 6 (online informational elaboration).

xiv *Introduction*

Mikhail Mikhailov works on a corpus-based analysis of six Russian translations of *Animal Farm* by George Orwell. The chapter contains a survey of methods to find which words are typical of one text as opposed to another, such as the Keywords utility on WordSmith Tools (Scott & Tribble, 2006) and Kilgarriff's (2009) measure. There is also a review of methods of studying similarity between texts by comparing their lexicons. This includes a novel suggestion for measuring the similarity of texts in different languages – by comparing a machine-translated version of the original English text to each of the translations. Once a matrix of inter-textual similarities has been created, it is possible to use multidimensional scaling (MDS), which produced a visual representation of which texts are similar and which are not. The author backs up the empirical findings with a qualitative comparison of the machine-translated original and each of the six translations.

Costa, Ferreira, Pagano and Meira explore semantic annotations to measure post-editing quality in machine translations. They base this research on the premise that the semantic relations found in the meanings of the source text add to its complexity, hence the difficulty of machine translation and thus the quality of the post-edited target language output. Other measures of source language complexity are semantic domain, number of sentences and numbers of pronouns. The importance of each of these factors in determining the final post-editing quality was found by logistic regression, using the WebNLG corpus of English–Portuguese post-edited translations. The two semantic categories most likely to have an impact on translation quality were comic characters (yielding better translations) and food (giving poorer translations).

Melania Cabezas-Garcia writes about analysing multiword terms such as "fixed-pitch wind turbine" in a specialised English corpus on ecology as a means to facilitate translation. Multiword terms (MWTs) are very important in imparting precise meaning in the technical domain, but their analysis is extremely complex. It is first necessary to find examples of MWT in the text, then structurally disambiguate them into the head and its modifiers, perform semantic analysis by placing the constituent words into ontology categories, and finally specify the relations between the words using a grammar based on Fillmore's (1982) FrameNet. Each of these steps is described clearly in detail, and then the author shows how the analysis of these "microcontexts" helps the translation of technical terms from English to Spanish.

Michael Oakes and Meng Ji

Notes

All references in the Introduction can be found in the individual chapters discussed.

1 See https://andreanini.com
2 See http://corpora.lancs.ac.uk/stats/index.php

1 A corpus-based analysis of medical communication

Euphemism as a communication strategy for context-specific responses

Sonia Asmahène Halimi, Razieh Azari, Pierrette Bouillon, and Hervé Spechbach

1 Background

As a specialty within medicine concerned with the development and delivery of emergency medical care, emergency medicine is viewed as an integrated body "of medical knowledge and skills concerning the acute phases of all types of disease and injury" (Arnold & Corte, 2003, p. 1). Many studies highlighted the high stress, unpredictability and time-critical context of emergency health care (Slade et al., 2015) that make emergency services particularly interruption-driven and multitasked (Burley, 2011; Chisholm et al., 2000). In addition, medical doctors (henceforth doctors) in emergency health care are not familiar with patients they meet, do not possess prior information on their social and medical background and do not know what languages they speak (Cox & Li, 2020). Today, it is a proven fact that emergency medicine is characterized by constraints that are increasingly challenging efficient provider–patient communication. Indeed, research findings documented significant issues that render communication in emergency departments "complex, nuanced and fragile" (Pun et al., 2015, p. 1). More concretely, communication with patients in emergency services "is threatened by time constraints, operational variation, crowding and boarding, excessive ambient noise, and other factors" (Maniya & McGreevy, 2020, p. 269). Slade et al. (2015) elaborated on the crucial role of communication in different stages of interaction with patients in emergencies, starting from the triage stage to the handover between doctors and passing by medical consultation and disposition. They identified the interpersonal parameter as a risk factor in patient safety, as emergency care relies heavily on spoken communication between patients and doctors (Slade et al., 2015). This risk factor can be aggravated by difficulties in communication due to language barriers (Burley, 2011; Cox & Li, 2020), which in turn can

DOI: 10.4324/9781003102694-1

result in medical errors (Bagchi et al., 2011; Eisenberg et al., 2005; Flores et al., 2003).

In response to communication difficulties in cross-cultural clinical settings (Kagawa-Singer and Kassim-Lakha, 2003; Priebe et al., 2011), several methods have been used for bridging the language barrier. They range from training or hiring bilingual health professionals to using remote language service (Hornberger et al., 1996). More recent solutions include speech translation systems (Albrecht et al., 2013) in assisting medical professionals in busy emergency services, such as Google Translate (Chang et al., 2014; Randhawa et al., 2013; Taylor et al., 2015), or speech-enabled medical phraselators, for instance BabelDr (Bouillon et al., 2017; Rayner et al., 2018; Spechbach et al., 2019), which are fixed-phrase translators.

The BabelDr speech-enabled phraselator is designed for real world medical communication, specifically to assist in reliable triaging of non-French-speaking patients in a preliminary medical examination dialogue. It can be conceptualized as a translation memory of relevant medical questions and instructions; the intention is that the doctor can talk freely and the system will map the recognized sentence to the closest sentence, which, if approved by the doctor, will be translated and oralized for the patient (Mutal et al., 2019). This translation application has been developed in the context of the refugee crisis in order to assist medical professionals who are currently facing major difficulties in communicating with foreign patients in the busy emergency services. It supports translation from French to Arabic, Spanish, Tigrinya, Farsi, Dari, and Swiss French Sign Language (LSF-CH) and covers domains and sentences referring to specific areas including sexual health (Bouillon et al., 2016; Ji et al., 2020). A distinguishing feature of the BabelDr phraselator is that it can be developed rapidly and directly by domain experts (Rayner et al., 2016), that is, doctors. The translation of questions and instructions is performed by professional translators but non-medical domain experts – hence the rationale for comparing the system's questions and the doctors' input in real situations.

The present study focused on the Persian translations of the system, drawing on two cross-sectional analyses. First, it addressed the ways, in the triage phase, to ask questions in Persian referring to taboo-related areas, such as sexual health. The focus was on types of euphemism doctors used as a strategy of communication when referring to sensitive concepts. Second, it examined the output of the BabelDr phraselator in relation to the same questions. The overall objective of our study was to draw on doctors' input to consolidate the performance of the phraselator by contextualizing its output in Persian. Based on our conclusions, we gave some recommendations on how phraselators should translate in the context of medical dialogs. As an overarching goal, the study helped inform us about the ways doctors used communication strategies (CSs) to achieve a balance between communicating medical information and establishing and building rapport with their patients.

After taking a glance at types of language and cultural barriers that doctors face in emergency departments, we examined the notion of euphemism and its use as a CS in health care contexts. We then elaborated on types of euphemism that Persian-speaking doctors use as a linguistic strategy to attenuate potentially offensive impact of sensitive sentences. While comparing the collected corpora from the doctors and the output of the phraselator, under this section, we studied how doctors' feedback can contribute to contextualizing the phraselator and consequently enhancing its culturally sensitive output.

Based on the stated objectives, the following research questions guided the present study:

1 What type of strategies do Persian doctors use to ask patients sensitive questions in a primary interview?
2 What are differences between doctors' questions and the phraselator's questions in Persian?
3 How can the phraselator be consolidated to make its content more context-sensitive?

2 Language and cultural barriers in emergency services

Language barriers can be a major obstacle to doctor–patient communication, especially in hampering proper medical interview and history-taking (Burley, 2011). But language differences are not the only source of poor communication. Culture differences too are increasingly seen as a component of the new cross-cultural paradigm for medical practice (van Wieringen et al., 2002). Such a paradigm draws on an understanding of the role of culture as a fundamental parameter in medical care (Kagawa-Singer & Kassim-Lakha, 2003; McIntosh, 1989; Rowland, 2020). Van Wieringen's study showed that, in the absence of mutual understanding, consultations more often end in "non-compliance with the prescribed therapy" (van Wieringen et al., 2002, p. 1). Ayonrinde (2003) and Brown et al. (2016) went further and argue that sharing a language is not a guarantee for effective and skillful communication between a doctor and patient because of different codes for interpersonal relationships, privacy or nonverbal communication. Besides the cultural parameter, Ayonrinde (2003) underlined that patients have their norms and taboos when they come for a medical consultation. In general, health care communication is more effective when participants are sensitive to each other's contextualization cues (Gumperz, 1992). For a long time, the impact of the cultural parameter on the quality of care went unheeded and was often dismissed due to inadequate understanding of its role and necessity (Kagawa-Singer & Kassim-Lakha, 2003). Today, there are professionals and agencies using cultural competency as a means to reduce the risk of miscommunication in culturally discordant clinical encounters (Jackson, 1993). In such a case, what is expected from a culturally competent medical practice is the ability, in a culturally different setting, to "respectfully elicit from the patient and family the information needed to make an accurate diagnosis and negotiate mutually satisfactory goals for treatment" (Kagawa-Singer & Kassim-Lakha, 2003, p. 580). That type of sensitivity is positively correlated with improved health outcomes and improved patient satisfaction (Ayonrinde, 2003).

Continuing from this, recognizing and bridging cultural differences in delivering effective information in care-giving implies that doctors use culturally sensitive language. That equates to saying that doctors are aware that cultural and social restrictions may have an impact on communication, in particular in the way patients dodge culturally objectionable concepts. In particular, suitable use of linguistic cues is meant to counter words with unpleasant connotations, for instance taboo words (Allan & Burridge, 2006; Bussmann, 1998), which are viewed by Bussmann as words that are usually replaced by euphemisms because of religious, political or sexual reasons. Experience also suggests that euphemisms are used to soften the harsh language of medicine and protect the patient's feelings in a diagnosis situation (Swift et al., 2013; Tayler & Ogden, 2005).

From the translation perspective, it means that linguistic communication cues, such as euphemisms, are used to minimize the effect of embarrassing sequences. This is reached by finding a culturally sensitive substitute while transferring the referent meaning into the target context.

In a cross-cultural clinical triage, for instance, the emergence of a taboo subject may make it difficult to conduct the clinical triage and hence render history-taking challenging. Talking about sexual health, for example, is often uncomfortable and considered as a taboo subject (Allan & Burridge, 2006).

The literature on taboo language described the phenomenon as being part of every culture (Alkhatib, 1995; Qanbar, 2011). Scholars tended to determine common areas, such as disease, death, sex, politics or politeness, as trigging the use of euphemisms (Alkhasawneh, 2018; Allan & Burridge, 2006) with regard to social constraints. Linguistic taboos are seen as one of the aspects of language that reflect sociocultural constraints and extend across cultures (Alkhatib, 1995; Allan & Burridge, 2006).

For Persian speakers, fatal diseases, death and the holiness of persons or places are, according to Bakhtiar (2012), three fear-based taboos that are "usually talked about with too much care and highly euphemistically" (p. 9). Other diseases are subject to linguistic restrictions and referred to through euphemistic mechanism as "being in association to taboo body parts" (Bakhtiar, 2012, p. 10). With this in mind, it is interesting to see how issues difficult to talk about, such as sexual health, are addressed in Persian health care communication. Some studies have addressed taboo subjects across languages and ways to render potentially offensive expressions from one cultural reality to another (Bakhtiar, 2012; Farghal, 1995; Ghounane, 2014; Rabab'ah & Al-Qarni, 2012; Tamimi Sa'd, 2017). In that sense and within primary health care, this study investigated the ways doctors circumvent taboo words to perform clear and barrier-free interviews with patients, as taboo words may influence the process of assessment when both doctors and patients are reluctant to openly discuss sensitive health issues. The aim was to draw on doctors' output to consolidate translated health care material in Persian.

3 Euphemism as strategy of communication

3.1 Basic viewpoints

The analysis of euphemism and its classification have been addressed by researchers from different perspectives including linguistics and sociolinguistics (Allan & Burridge, 1991, 2006; Casas Gómez, 2009; Holder, 2002; Linfoot-Ham, 2005; Radulovic, 2016; Warren, 1992), translation studies (Bakhtiar, 2012; Farghal, 1995; Rabab'ah & Al-Qarni, 2012; Tamimi Sa'd, 2017) and medical discourse (Stewart, 2005; Tacheva, 2013; Weijts et al., 1993).

With regard to manifestations of euphemism in discourse, one of the best-known and most-quoted definitions of euphemism is provided by Allan and Burridge (1991), who described euphemism "as an alternative to a dispreferred expression" (p. 11) with the aim of preserving face. The authors emphasized the relative levels of politeness intended through the use of euphemisms, concluding that this strategy of politeness has a pragmatic dimension and depends on the context. Allan and Burridge (1991) provided one of the first models that represents ways in which euphemisms may be formed. They determined different types of euphemistic manifestations in discourse: remodeling, circumlocution, clipping, acronyms, abbreviation, omission, one-for-one substitution, general-for-specific, part-for-whole, learned terms, borrowing, hyperbole, understatement.

In keeping with the overall approach of Allan and Burridge (1991), Casas Gómez (2009) reviewed different definitions of euphemism and adopted a pragmatic approach as well, arguing that the euphemistic process is of a social nature with a contextual function. He described euphemism as the conceptualization of a forbidden reality with a view to attenuate that reality or concept, or, to reinforce it (Casas Gómez, 2009).

Among other definitions is Warren's (1992). She described euphemism as being structured around three main defining features; the sensitive connotation of the referent word, the soft aspect of the alternative word, and the awareness of interlocutors of the use of euphemistic mechanisms to avoid embarrassing words. Her approach helped us to understand the transfer of the connotative aspects in the referent and its alternative from the target-language perspective. The analysis presented led to a detailed classification of the ways in which euphemisms can be constructed, enumerating main euphemism formation ways, namely: (a) word formation devices; (b) phonemic modification; (c) loan words; and (d) semantic innovation.

For the purpose of this study, the classifications proposed by Allan and Burridge (1991) and Warren (1992) were used as the point of departure for analyzing the corpora. They adopted a pragmatic approach toward euphemism that is aligned with the purpose of the present study. These two classifications have some overlaps, but each has specific features which can complement one another. Examples of these two classifications were provided when analyzing doctors' strategies in communication.

3.2 Euphemisms in health communication

Because of changes in the perception of the notion of "patient" over the past decades, the patient is now regarded as a partner in the therapy (Coulter, 1999; Greene & Hibbard, 2012; Mead & Bower, 2002; Rathert et al., 2013; Santana et al., 2018). Thus, focus is on patient participation and involvement in the treatment in addition to the relationship and communication with health care professionals. Thus, medical best practices emphasize the significance of sociolinguistic factors in treatment outcomes, ranging from the deliberate selection of positive language to the attention given to cultural awareness and sensitivity, including patients' beliefs and values (Napier et al., 2017; de Gault et al., 2016; Kissane et al., 2017; Rowland, 2020). One of the sensitive verbal manifestations in the interaction between patients and health care professionals is the use of euphemism, identified by researchers as an effective communication technique when talking about sensitive issues.

The significance of euphemistic use in health care communication has been documented in many studies. Euphemism is used as a careful language to protect patients' feeling and reduce distress associated with critical medical conditions (Allan & Burridge, 2006; Jamet, 2018; Tacheva, 2013), including heart failure (Tayler & Ogden, 2005), obesity (Swift et al., 2013;

Tailor & Ogden, 2009), cancer (Epton et al., 2020), and death (Herbert, 2016). Euphemism is also employed to avoid taboo or explicit terminology when talking about sexual issues, for example in gynecological consultations (Stewart, 2005; Weijts et al., 1993) or sensitive health issues with adolescents (Harvey, 2013).

Ultimately, the deliberate choice to use or not use euphemism in doctor–patient communication depends on the doctor's understanding of the relevant factors. Not only is the perception of the offensive or sensitive nature context-driven and, therefore, sometimes difficult to assess (Allan & Burridge, 2006), researches considered such a discursive process as an evasive language. Referring to realities or medical concepts through euphemism contributes, in some scholars' views, to depersonalization and reinforces stereotypes, an aspect well illustrated by examples related to female sexuality, reproductive medicine, and bodily aspects (Sontag, 1978; Stewart, 2005; Weijts et al., 1993). Moreover, best practices in palliative conditions view the use of cautious language instead of explicitly expressed medical references as a source of confusion and lack of clarity in the medical discourse (Rodriguez et al., 2007). Euphemisms can also prevent the patient from understanding the serious nature of the case, specifically for life-threatening illnesses (Herbert, 2016).

Regardless of its multifaceted impact on health care communication, the role of euphemism as a strategy of communication around the subject of sexual issues should be thoroughly investigated in relation to translation. There would be much to gain in contextualizing discourse on sexual health by adopting doctors' communication cues when transferring concepts from one cultural context to another. Contextualization was related here to Persian sensitive questions and instructions asked by doctors and the way translation could benefit from strategies used by them.

3.3 Euphemisms in Persian health communication

Although a few studies have examined the use of euphemism in Persian discourse, we are not aware of any study that has investigated euphemism specifically in Persian health communication. In his study focused on communicative functions of euphemisms in Persian, Bakhtiar (2012) explained that "applying medical jargons and circumlocutions are common ways" (p. 9) in Persian communication to avoid referring directly to taboo-related diseases. For example, the word *HIV mosbat* (literal translation (LT): HIV positive) is used in Persian to refer euphemistically to *eidz* (LT: AIDS). Similarly, the word *kanser* (LT: cancer) is used to refer to *saratan* (LT: cancer) (Bakhtiar, 2012). He explained that diseases related to taboo body parts are euphemized as well. For example, the words *suzak* (LT: gonorrhea)

8 Sonia Asmahène Halimi et al.

and *siflis* (LT: syphilis) are replaced by *amraz e mogharebati* (LT: intercourse diseases). It should be mentioned that Bakhtiar's study focused on euphemism in Persian generally, not on Persian health communication specifically. It is also noteworthy to point out that there are some studies focused on sexual health education in Iran such as Latifnejad Roudsari et al. (2013), MirzaiiNajmabadi et al. (2019), Mosavi et al. (2014) and Askari et al. (2020). However, these studies mainly investigated challenges to sexual health education and did not work on euphemism in health communication specifically.

4 Study of euphemism in primary medical interviews in Persian language

4.1 Study objective

The research divided into two pieces. The first cross-sectional analysis focused on the ways doctors ask questions in Persian in the primary interview with regard to sexual health and technical questions associated with sexual health and bodily functions. Based on previous studies (Swift et al., 2013; Tayler & Ogden, 2005), we argued that euphemisms were preferred by doctors as a strategy of communication to attenuate the connotation of delicate words considered as taboo in the given context.

The second cross-sectional analysis assessed the corpus collected with the doctors and the phraselator corpus in Persian. It suggested that the distinctive nuances of compared data seem significant enough to consolidate the speech-enabled phraselator BabelDr on the basis of the doctors' input. This application, which supports speech recognition and productive use of language and speech recognition, could then be improved by reliable and context-sensitive data.

4.1.1 Corpus

For the purpose of this study, 20 sensitive Persian sentences (medical questions) were extracted from the BabelDr. They were selected based on the following criteria:

1 Sexual health: Sentences contain references to sex-related organs, diseases, examinations and tests.
2 Bodily functions: Sentences contain words and phrases relating to other sensitive bodily functions, such as "urinate", "bowel movement", "emit gas".

Table 1.1 Selected sentences representing defined criteria

Criteria	Sentence
Sexual health	آیا مشکل پروستات دارید؟
	LT: Do you have prostate problems?
Bodily functions	آیا امروز مَدفوع کرده اید؟
	LT: Have you had faeces today?

These criteria were used in Azari et al. (2019). Table 1.1 illustrates sentences representing each criterion.

Doctors who are all Persian native speakers were asked to read each sentence and provide the versions that they would use in a real-life situation. They were specifically requested to ask the sensitive questions as they would do when addressing a Persian-speaking patient in a primary care consultation. The doctors were asked to give all versions they would use in real life for each question. They all gave randomly different versions. This resulted in two corpora; one produced by the doctors and one produced by the nonmedical translator. Detailed profiles of the doctors and the data analysis procedure are discussed in the following sections.

4.1.2 Participants

To build the export-produced corpus, a group of ten doctors who are all Persian native speakers living and working in Iran were asked to participate in the study. Six doctors, including three men and three women, agreed to participate. All male doctors were general practitioners (GPs). Two of the female doctors were gynecologists, and one was a general surgeon.

For the phraselator corpus, Persian sentences were translated by the same non-expert translator, a Persian native speaker, following a defined process of translation: translation, revision and correction. The translator was asked to provide one translation in Persian for each question in French. Documentary and terminological research was conducted, and resources used in order to find relevant information and produce accurate translations. Some questions were presented to the translator along with comments and explanations to avoid ambiguity and misunderstanding regarding the intended purpose of the question. Additionally, core questions were given to the translator along with variants in order to make the questions as unambiguous and explicit as possible. For example, a question such as "Do you have fever?" is presented together with "Do you feel you're running a temperature?" or "Do you have a temperature?" Similarly, the question "Which way is the pain going?" is associated with the variant "Could you show me with your finger the direction in which the pain is radiating?" In the range of questions related to sexual health, the core question "Have you had a breast biopsy?" has the variants: "Did you go through a breast biopsy recently?" or "Have you ever had a breast biopsy?" For an enquiry about a rectal touch examination, the sentence "Have you had a rectal examination" is associated with "Have you been examined by rectal touch?" For menstruation, the question "Are you on your menstrual cycle right now?" is associated with "Have you got your period now?"

It must be noted, however, that variants provided in the phraselator corpus with regard to sexual health are not well developed, at least not enough to provide contextualized solutions. Except for a few examples where variants to the core question are formed by euphemism, for example, a camera in the bladder for cystoscopy or erectile dysfunctions and impotence problems for erection problems, most sentences considered as variants do not include contextualized words or phrases that are substituted for medical terms that may raise a taboo subject (sex organs, sexual intercourses or bodily functions, etc.). It is clear that they cannot be enough to ease the transfer of medical concepts to the target communication situation and signal the relevant aspect in the new context.

4.1.3 Analysis

To identify and categorize CSs used by the doctors and the nonmedical translator, the two corpora, that is, sentences produced by the doctors and sentences translated by the translator for the phraselator, were analyzed carefully. Based on the classifications proposed by Allan and Burridge (1991) and Warren (1992), a Persian native speaker carried out an annotation that was consolidated by a second native speaker. A third evaluator corroborated the annotation. Each strategy used to circumvent questions associated with the defined criteria, that is, sexual health and bodily functions, was identified and classified. We identified *paraphrasing* and *using formal words* (Table 1.2) as two other CSs used by the doctors to circumvent sensitive concepts. The main CSs found in the two corpora are reported in Table 1.2 and Table 1.3 together with frequencies of occurrence.

4.1.3.1 STRATEGIES PERSIAN DOCTORS USED TO ASK SENSITIVE QUESTIONS

According to Table 1.2, three CSs were used by the doctors: euphemism, with its different types, plus using formal words and using paraphrase. In total, eight different types of euphemism were identified: using transliteration (loan words), implication, deletion, metonymy, ellipsis, part-for-whole + ellipsis, using transliteration (loan words) + general-for-specific and

Table 1.2 Communication strategies used by the doctors

Communication strategy		Criteria		Total
		Sexual health	Bodily functions	
Euphemism	Using transliteration (loan words)	31	0	31
	Implication	23	6	29
	Deletion	10	0	10
	Metonymy	0	10	10
	Total	64	16	80
Using formal words		72	33	105
Using paraphrase		35	0	35

particularization, which were used in 83 instances. Table 1.2 represents the most common euphemism types only.

When communicating around sexual health, the doctors have most frequently resorted to euphemism specifically, using transliteration (loan words) (31 instances), implication (23 instances), and deletion (10 instances). The following examples illustrated the use of each euphemistic category as a strategy for avoiding taboo-related sensitive concepts.

4.1.3.1.1 Using transliteration As Allan and Burridge (1991) and Warren (1992) stated, importing or borrowing foreign words is one of the ways in which euphemisms can be constructed, for example, "anus" and "rectum" from Latin. Based on Allan and Burridge (1991) and Warren (1992), cases where the doctors used foreign words to communicate around sexual health were considered as transliteration (loan words). In the following examples, the Persian sentences provided to the doctors (Question) and the Persian versions provided by the doctors and their LTs are presented. The words "condom" and "period" were borrowed, and their transliterated forms were used.

Examples:

Question 1: Do you use <u>a condom</u>?
Doctor's version in Persian:

کنید؟ آیا شما از <u>کاندوم</u> استفاده می

LT: Do you use <u>a condom</u>?
Question 2: Are you on your <u>monthly cycle</u> now?
Doctor's version in Persian:

الان <u>پریود</u> هستین؟

LT: Are you on your <u>period</u> now?

12 Sonia Asmahène Halimi et al.

Bakhtiar (2012) referred to use of transliterated words in Persian such as *seks* (sex) used in Persian to refer to sexual intercourse instead of the Persian phrase *rabeteh jensi* (LT: Sexual relation). As Allan (2016) mentioned, "using words borrowed from other languages to function as euphemisms is characteristic of many languages" (p. 9). "French and Latin have long been sources for English euphemisms" (Allan & Burridge, 2006, p. 201). For example, in English, words for bodily effluvia, sex and the associated acts are Latin-based, for example, defecate instead of shit, copulate instead of fuck and genitals instead of sex organs (Allan, 2016). Several reasons could be considered for this selection. Bakhtiar (2012) stated that sexual matters are among the most censored areas in Persian. As he explained, avoiding possible loss of interlocutors' face is a motivating factor for using euphemism in these cases. Embarrassment, shame and being less offensive could be possible reasons for using foreign words.

4.1.3.1.2 Implication Implication was the other strategy that the doctors used to create euphemisms when they were communicating around sexual health. By implication we here mean the use of general words to refer to specific concepts in a definite context. Implication in Warren's (1992) terms corresponds to referents that are frequently concomitant and related to a context and conventional usage; that is, if X (old referent) is valid, then (probably) Y (new referent) is valid too e.g. "*sleeping with someone* ('having sexual intercourse with somebody')" (p. 131). Warren (1992) believed that implications are vague, as the listener can only interpret them based on circumstantial evidence. In the following examples, "chest" and "front" were used in Persian to refer to "breast" and "genitals", respectively.

Examples:

Question 3: Have you ever done breast biopsy?
Doctor's version in Persian:

تا حالا پزشک از سینه های شما برای
تشخیص بیماری نمونه گرفته است؟

LT: Has doctor ever taken a sample of your chest for diagnosis?
Question 4: Do your genitals swell?
Doctor's version in Persian:

آیا جلو شما ورم دارد؟

LT: Does your front have swelling?

In Persian, "behind" and "front" are used to euphemistically refer to "buttocks" and "female sexual organs", respectively (Bakhtiar, 2012). Weijts et al.

(1993) observed that physicians used terms such as "down there" to refer to the vagina when talking about sexuality with patients. Avoiding loss of face, shame and being less offensive could be reasons for selecting this strategy.

4.1.3.1.3 Deletion According to Allan and Burridge (1991) and Warren (1992), euphemism can be achieved through deletion. The offensive words and phrases can be deleted (Warren, 1992). Based on Allan and Burridge (1991) and Warren (1992), cases where the doctors did not use words and phrases relating to sexual health were considered as deletion. In the following examples, the word "prostate" was deleted.

Examples:

Question 5: Do you have prostate problems?
Doctor's version in Persian:
آیا ادرار قطره قطره داری؟
LT: Do you have drip by drip urine?
Doctor's version in Persian:
شبها چند بار از خواب برای ادرار کردن بیدار می شوید؟
LT: During the night, do you wake up several times to urinate?

Weijts et al. (1993) observed total omission of delicate terms as a strategy that physicians use when talking about sexuality with patients. They said that discussing sexual health often seems difficult and embarrassing for physicians and patients. Avoiding loss of face, shame and being less offensive could be other possible reasons.

The doctors used formal words and phrases and paraphrasing as other CSs that were not enumerated as euphemism categories by Warren (1992) and Allan and Burridge (1991).

4.1.3.1.4 Using formal words Using formal words and phrases generally appear in press and formal situations. In the case of speaking, formal language is usually used for official or serious situations (Levin et al., 1994). It was the other dominant CS that the doctors used when communicating around sexual health. This CS can be associated with what Allan and Burridge (2006) called *orthophemism*. They defined *orthophemism* as direct words or phrases that are neither pleasant nor offensive. It is used an alternative to a dispreferred expression "that is not the preferred, desired or appropriate expression" (Allan & Burridge, 2006, p. 32). In the following examples, some of the doctors used formal phrases in Persian to refer to "oral sex" and "sexual desire" respectively.

Examples:

Question 6: Have you had <u>oral sexual relations</u>?
Doctor's version in Persian:
آیا رابطه جنسی دهانی داشته اید؟
LT: Have you had *oral* sexual relations?
Question 7: Has your <u>sexual desire</u> decreased?
Doctor's version in Persian:
میل جنسی شما کم شده است؟
LT: Has your <u>libido</u> decreased?

In these examples, the Persian words and phrases used to refer to oral sex and sexual desire are generally used in press and formal situations. Generally, formal language is motivated by conditions such as keeping social distance and showing competency and capability (Levin et al., 1994). Formal words and phrases, that is, *orthophemism* "avoid possible loss of face by the speaker, and also the hearer or some third party" (Allan & Burridge, 2006). There is another possible reason that can be pointed at: Being on the safe side. Comparing with other CSs (loan words, deletion, etc.), using formal words and phrases to communicate around sexual health may help doctors to provide patients with proper amount of information while at the same time avoiding loss of face. Shame and being less offensive could be other explanations.

4.1.3.1.5 Using paraphrase Paraphrasing and explaining technical terms in simple words was the other dominant CS that the doctors used when talking about sexual health to patients. This CS was mainly used to replace technical terms such as "colonoscopy", "mammography", "cystoscopy", etc. In the following example, "cystoscopy" was replaced by "an examination of your bladder and urinary tract with a device".

Example:

Sentence 8: We will do a <u>cystoscopy</u>.
Doctor's version in Persian:
مجاری ادراری شما توسط دستگاه انجام خواهیم داد.
ما یک بررسی از مثانه و
LT: We will do <u>an examination of your bladder and urinary tract with a device</u>.

Using less medical and technical jargon, as recommended by previous studies including Graham and Brookey (2008), Pitt and Hendrickson (2020) and Farrington (2011), could be one reason for using this CS. It was observed that the doctors were keen to paraphrase medical terms when deemed necessary despite the fact that they could resort to formal language too.

The applied CSs analyzed here, specifically ways of euphemism formation and formal words and phrases, have shown that communication around sexual health is highly sensitive from the point of view of Persian doctors. Previous studies, Brown et al. (2006), Traumer et al. (2019), Serrant-Green (2005), Stewart (2005), Weijts et al. (1993), etc. have shown that this point of view is, unsurprisingly, in no way exclusive to Persian doctors.

Regarding bodily functions, the results showed that the doctors have used CSs such as formal words and metonymy more often to refer to words and phrases such as "urinate", "bowel movement", "emit gas", etc. Instead of referring to the specific concept, they tended to employ substitutes that are closely associated. As Warren (1992) stated, we have a metonym "if a word is applied to referents which are not in the conventional set of this word but which are connected with the conventional referents in one of the [following] ways": causal, whole-part, locative, and equative relations (p. 149). The following example represented use of metonymy by the doctors.
Example:

Question 9: Have you had faeces today?
Doctor's version in Persian:

آیا امروز شکمت کار کرده؟

LT: Has your stomach worked today?

It seems that talking about bodily functions were considered sensitive by Persian doctors, as evidenced by the applied CSs discussed previously. "Go to the toilet" is used euphemistically to refer to "urinate" and/or "defecate" (Warren, 1992). This is a vague phrase. However, the patient might understand the exact meaning depending on doctor's questions that precede the passage and the patient's health problems.

For both areas, sexual health and bodily functions, the results showed that in some cases, all the doctors or most of them used one similar strategy to formulate versions of one sentence. For example, to provide versions of "Do you have erection problems?" all the doctors opted for paraphrasing. To ask the following question – "Have you had faeces today?" – all the doctors, except one, resorted to a similar strategy, metonymy, to enquire about faeces. Sometimes, they acted differently and used various strategies for the same sentence. For example, the doctors opted for four different strategies to provide versions of "Have you ever had a digital rectal examination?" They asked the following questions: "Have you ever been examined from behind?" "Has any doctor ever examined your anal

16 Sonia Asmahène Halimi et al.

Table 1.3 Communication strategies used by the nonmedical translator

Communication strategy		Criteria		Total
		Sexual health	Bodily functions	
Euphemism	Using transliteration (loan words)	12	0	12
	Total	12	0	12
Using formal words		21	10	31

area for a problem that you have had?" or "Have you been examined through the anus with finger?"

According to Table 1.3, the nonmedical translator used two CSs, euphemism and using formal words. The results showed that words and phrases referring to sexual health were considered as highly sensitive by the nonmedical translator. The dominant strategy employed in this corpus was using formal words. As well as the fear of transferring taboo concepts in the target context, avoiding confusion and mistakes could be the main reason for this selection. Comparing with other CSs such as loan words, deletion, etc., using formal words and phrases to communicate around sexual health is safer, as it does not lose information.

The other dominant strategy used by the nonmedical translator to formulate translations related to sexual health was transliteration or using loan words. It was observed that this CS was mainly used to deal with technical terms such as "colonoscopy", "mammography", "cystoscopy", etc. Less familiarity with medical jargon and avoiding confusion, mistakes and lengthy sentences could be considered as possible reasons for this selection.

To refer to bodily functions, the nonmedical translator employed only one CS, using formal words. This shows that these words and phrases were considered sensitive by the Persian nonmedical translator. Again, avoiding possible confusion and mistakes could be the main reason.

In contrast to the two previous CSs used by the nonmedical translator, the phraselator corpus does not contain euphemistic expressions resulting from implication, metonymy, deletion or paraphrasing.

4.1.3.2 DIFFERENCES BETWEEN DOCTORS AND THE PHRASELATOR'S QUESTIONS IN PERSIAN

When analyzing the corpus produced by the Persian doctors, it becomes evident that words and phrases referring to sexual health have a high level of sensitivity, as the main CSs the Persian doctors used to communicate around sexual health are euphemism and using formal words. The Persian nonmedical translator used only two CSs to take into account the sensitive question of sexual health in translation, that is, using transliteration (12 instances) and using formal words (21 instances).

While paraphrasing and explaining technical terms in simple words was the other dominant CS that the doctors used when talking about sexual health to patients, the nonmedical translator did not apply this strategy at all. The doctors mainly used this CS to replace technical terms such as "colonoscopy", "mammography", "cystoscopy", etc. In the same context, the nonmedical translator acted differently and opted for loan words. Less familiarity with medical jargon, avoiding mistakes, confusion and lengthy sentences could be possible reasons for opting for loan words.

Comparing with other CSs employed by the doctors, the nonmedical translator's use of formal words and phrases seems safer, as it does not lose of information and keeps the target language closer to the original question, instead of opting for naturalness and ease.

Strategies employed in both corpora to communicate sentences of the second criterion have shown that the doctors and the nonmedical translator considered words and phrases such as "urinate", "bowel movement", "emit gas", etc., sensitive too. Beside using formal words and phrases, the doctors used implication and metonymy to talk about bodily functions, while the nonmedical translator used formal words and phrases only. Avoiding confusion and mistakes could be considered as the main reason for the nonmedical translator's decision.

Comparing the two corpora has shown that the doctors have used more diverse CSs. Some of the CSs used by the doctors have been the same as the nonmedical translator's, and some have been different (implication, deletion, etc.). The CSs employed by the nonmedical translator could be more diverse if the gathered corpus was based on translations produced by more than one translator or interpreter.

Overall, most strategies opted for by the Persian doctors to ask questions related to sexual health correspond with the strategies reported by previous studies done in different languages and culture. It seems reasonable to hope that the findings of this study can be considered as relevant to other languages.

4.1.3.3 CONSOLIDATING THE PHRASELATOR

In verifying the original research questions, the analysis of the two corpora, the doctors' and the phraselator's corpora, it becomes evident that words and phrases referring to sexual health have a high level of sensitivity; the main CSs the Persian doctors have used to communicate around sexual health are euphemisms and using formal words. It could plausibly be argued that the doctors' approach stems from a better understanding of the real-life medical context. On the other hand, only two strategies used in the phraselator's corpus produced by the Persian nonmedical translator directly reflect that sensitivity. Apart from the recourse to transliteration and formal expressions, the translator's approach to handling sexual health questions is form-focused and less euphemistic. Less familiarity with medical jargon, caution and less insight into the conventions of medical examination dialogues could be reasons for restricting the transfer of medical concepts in the phraselator to transliteration and formal words. For this reason, the data gathered from the doctors may be of value in consolidating the phraselator.

The doctors easily find strategies to explain technical concepts in different ways, for example by paraphrasing. The variant formulations that are not found in the phraselator can be integrated to it as variants.

While the BabelDr phraselator is beginning to establish itself as a reliable application for carrying out interlingual medical examination dialogues, with a source language coverage that is continuously and directly developed by French domain experts, this study suggests that coverage in Persian, particularly in relation to sensitive questions, could be mapped to variants that build on a corpus with questions collected from target language doctors. Those variants are, then, used as aid tools for the translation process. As a matter of fact, it has been shown that questions related to sensitive matters cannot be translated literally. Their translation involves medical knowledge and entails an appropriate reformulation or explanation. In that sense, euphemistic phrases used by the doctors could be given to translators as additional tools to identify sensitive questions and translate them appropriately. Domain experts or translators could also be asked to systematically note problematic sentences and proposed translations so that the strategies used can be validated and, possibly, shared between languages. Indeed, medical dialogues include a verbal dimension that should be present in the translated text. This is possible when the strategies the Persian doctors used to ask questions are taken into consideration in developing the phraselator corpus.

Conclusion

Studies carried out by many researchers have suggested that communication around the subject of sexual health is one of the most sensitive and challenging areas in health communication. As Stewart (2005) stated, sexual health and related topics are taboo and do not fit comfortably into language use. The validity of this point of view is entirely consistent with the data from the Persian medical doctors that we describe here. Moreover, studies in health communication (Ayonrinde, 2003; Brown, 2016; Rowland, 2020) asserted the role of cultural sensitivity to insure effective and accurate communication and therefore positive health outcomes. The present study tried to categorize the communication strategies (CSs) that Persian doctors employ in primary examination to deliver sensitive questions related to taboo subjects such as sexual health and bodily functions, extracted from the BabelDr phraselator.

The study findings showed that the doctors are more confident in using a diverse range of CSs to talk about sensitive matters compared to those currently used for the Persian target language coverage in the BabelDr phraselator. Resorting to different types of euphemism to communicate around sensitive matters with patients was one of the dominant strategies that they used. These applied CSs can profitably be studied by translators and interpreters to have a better understanding of real-life situations before they need to face them.

Considering the differences between the two Persian corpora, it seems reasonable to argue that considering the CSs used by medical doctors could help develop a consolidated phraselator corpus that is better able to handle culturally sensitive contexts. In this sense, core translated sentences can be complemented by translation variants from the doctors' output to make medical dialogs more relevant and closer to reality.

In conclusion, we hope that this corpus-based study will in general have useful implications for the translation of culturally sensitive medical primary examination dialogues.

References

Albrecht, U. V., Behrends, M., Schmeer, R., Matthies, H. K., & von Jan, U. (2013). Usage of multilingual mobile translation applications in clinical settings. *JMIR mHealth and uHealth*, *1*(1), e4. https://doi.org/10.2196/mhealth.2268

Alkhasawneh, F. (2018). An international study of euphemistic strategies used in Saudi Arabic and American English. *Indonesian Journal of Applied Linguistics*, *8*(1), 217–225. doi: 10.17509/ijal.v8i1.11466

Alkhatib, M. (1995). A sociolinguistic view of linguistic taboo in Jordanian Arabic. *Journal of Multilingual and Multicultural Development*, *16*(6), 443–457. https://doi.org/10.1080/01434632.1995.9994617

Allan, K. (2016). Pragmatics in language change and lexical creativity. *SpringerPlus*, *5*, 342. https://doi.org/10.1186/s40064-016-1836-y

Allan, K., & Burridge, K. (1991). *Euphemism and dysphemism: Language used as a shield and weapon*. Oxford: Oxford University Press.

Allan, K., & Burridge, K. (2006). *Forbidden words: Taboo and the censoring of language*. Cambridge: Cambridge University Press. https://doi.org/10.1017/CBO9780511617881

Arnold, J. L., & Corte, D. F. (2003). International emergency medicine: Recent trends and future challenges. *European Journal of Emergency Medicine: Official Journal of the European Society for Emergency Medicine*, *10*(3), 180–188. https://doi.org/10.1097/00063110-200309000-00005

Askari, F., Mirzaiinajmabadi, K., Saeedy Rezvani, M., & Asgharinekah, S. M. (2020). Sexual health education issues (challenges) for adolescent boys in Iran: A qualitative study. *Journal of Education and Health Promotion*, *9*, 33. https://doi.org/10.4103/jehp.jehp_462_19

Ayonrinde, O. (2003). Importance of cultural sensitivity in therapeutic transactions. *Disease Management & Health Outcomes*, *11*, 233–248. https://doi.org/10.2165/00115677-200311040-00004

Azari, R., Bouillon, P., Gerlach, J., Spechbach, H., & Halimi, S. (2019). Using crowdsourcing to evaluate lay-friendliness of BabelDr. In S. Mikkonen (Ed.), *Proceedings of conference on easy-to-read language research* (KLAARA 2019) (p. 6). University of Helsinki. www.helsinki.fi/sites/default/files/atoms/files/final_book_of_abstracts_klaara_180919.pdf

Bagchi, A. D., Dale, S., Verbitsky-Savitz, N., Andrecheck, S., Zavotsky, K., & Eisenstein, R. (2011). Examining effectiveness of medical interpreters in emergency departments for Spanish-speaking patients with limited English proficiency: Results of a randomized controlled trial. *Annals of Emergency Medicine*, *57*(3), 248–256.e4. https://doi.org/10.1016/j.annemergmed.2010.05.032

Bakhtiar, M. (2012). Communicative functions of euphemisms in Persian. *The Journal in International Social Research*, *5*(20), 7–12.

Bouillon, P., Gerlach, J., Spechbach, H., Tsourakis, N., & Halimi, S. (2017). BabelDr vs Google Translate: A user study at Geneva University Hospitals (HUG). In *The 20th annual conference of the european association for machine translation* (pp. 47–52). https://ufal.mff.cuni.cz/eamt2017/user-project-product-papers/Conference_Booklet_EAMT2017.pdf

Bouillon, P., Spechbach, H., Durieux-Paillard, S., Gerlach, J., Halimi Mallem, I. S., Hudelson, P., . . . Tsourakis, N. (2016). *BabelDr: A web platform for rapid construction of phrasebook-style medical speech translation applications*. https://archive-ouverte.unige.ch/unige:83843

Brown, B., Crawford, P., & Carter, R. (2006). *Evidence-based health communication*. Maidenhead: Open University Press.

Brown, E., Bekker, H., Davidson, S., Koffman, J., & Schell, J. (2016). Supportive care: Communication strategies to improve cultural competence in shared decision making. *Clinical Journal of the American Society of Nephrology*, *11*(10), 1902–1908. https://doi.org/10.2215/CJN.13661215

Burley, D. (2011). Better communication in the emergency department. *Emergency Nurse: The Journal of the RCN Accident and Emergency Nursing Association*, *19*(2), 32–36. https://doi.org/10.7748/en2011.05.19.2.32.c8509

Bussmann, H. (1998). *Routledge dictionary of language and linguistics*. Abingdon, UK: Routledge.

Casas Gómez, M. (2009). Towards a new approach to the linguistic definition of euphemism. *Language Science*, *31*(2009), 725–739. https://doi.org/10.1016/j.langsci.2009.05.001

Chang, D. T., Thyer, I. A., Hayne, D., & Katz, D. J. (2014). Using mobile technology to overcome language barriers in medicine. *Annals of the Royal College of Surgeons of England*, *96*(6), e23–e25. https://doi.org/10.1308/0035884 14X13946184903685

Chisholm, C. D., Collison, E. K., Nelson, D. R., & Cordell, W. H. (2000). Emergency department workplace interruptions: Are emergency physicians "interrupt-driven" and "multitasking"? *Academic Emergency Medicine: Official Journal of the Society for Academic Emergency Medicine*, *7*(11), 1239–1243. https://doi.org/10.1111/j.1553-2712.2000.tb00469.x

Coulter, A., Entwistle, V., & Gilbert, D. (1999). Sharing decisions with patients: Is the information good enough? *BMJ (Clinical Research Ed.)*, *318*(7179), 318–322. https://doi.org/10.1136/bmj.318.7179.318

Cox, A., & Li, S. (2020). The medical consultation through the lenses of language and social interaction theory. *Advances in Health Sciences Education: Theory and Practice*, *25*(1), 241–257. https://doi.org/10.1007/s10459-018-09873-2

De Gault, I., Shapcott, J., Luthi, A., & Graeme, R. (2016). *Communication in nursing and healthcare: A guide for compassionate practice*. Thousand Oaks, CA: Sage Publication Inc.

Eisenberg, E. M., Murphy, A. G., Sutcliffe, K., Wears, R., Schenkel, S., Perry, S., & Vanaerhoef, M. (2005). Communication in emergency medicine: Implications for patient safety. *Communication Monographs*, *72*(4), 390–413. https://doi.org/10.1080/03637750500322602

Epton, T., Chittem, M., Tanikella, R., Rajappa, S., Sinha, S., & Harris, P. (2020). Indian patient use of cancer euphemisms: Association with psychological outcomes and health behaviours. *Psycho-Oncology*, *29*, 1193–1200. https://doi.org/10.1002/pon.5408

Farghal, M. (1995). Euphemism in Arabic: A Gricean interpretation. *Anthropological Linguistics*, *37*(3), 366–378.

Farrington, C. (2011). Reconciling managers, doctors, and patients: The role of clear communication. *Journal of the Royal Society of Medicine*, *104*(6), 231–236. https://doi.org/10.1258/jrsm.2011.100401

Flores, G., Laws, M. B., Mayo, S. J., Zuckerman, B., Abreu, M., Medina, L., & Hardt, E. J. (2003). Errors in medical interpretation and their potential clinical consequences in pediatric encounters. *Pediatrics*, *111*(1), 6–14. https://doi.org/10.1542/peds.111.1.6

Gerlach, J., Spechbach, H., & Bouillon, P. (2019). Creating an online translation platform to build target language resources for a medical phraselator. In D. Chambers, J. Drugan, J. Esteves-Ferreira, J. M. Macan, R. Mitkov, & O. M. Stefanov (Eds.), *Proceedings of the 40th conference translating and the computer* (pp. 60–65). AsLing, The International Association for Advancement in Language Technology. www.asling.org/tc40/wp-content/uploads/TC40-Proceedings.pdf

Ghounane, N. (2014). A sociolinguistic view of linguistic taboos and euphemistic strategies in the Algerian society: Attitudes and beliefs in Tlemcen speech community. *IMPACT: International Journal of Research in Applied, Natural and Social Sciences*, *2*(3), 73–88.

Graham, S., & Brookey, J. (2008). Do patients understand? *The Permanente Journal*, *12*(3), 67–69. https://doi.org/10.7812/tpp/07-144
Greene, J., & Hibbard, J. H. (2012). Why does patient activation matter? An examination of the relationships between patient activation and health-related outcomes. *Journal of General Internet Medicine*, *27*(5), 520–526. doi: 10.1007/s11606-011-1931-2
Gumperz, J. (1992). Contextualization and understanding. In A. Duranti & C. Goodwin (Eds.), *Rethinking context* (pp. 229–252). Cambridge: Cambridge University Press. https://web.stanford.edu/~eckert/PDF/gumperz1992.pdf
Harvey, K. (2013). *Investigating adolescent health communication: A corpus linguistics approach*. London: Bloomsbury Academic.
Herbert, A. (2016). The role of euphemisms in healthcare communication. *Journal of Healthcare Communication*, *1*(2). doi: 10.4172/2472-1654.100014
Holder, R. (2002). *How not to say what you mean: A dictionary of euphemisms*. Oxford: Oxford University Press.
Hornberger, J. C., Gibson, C. D., Jr, Wood, W., Dequeldre, C., Corso, I., Palla, B., & Bloch, D. A. (1996). Eliminating language barriers for non-English-speaking patients. *Medical Care*, *34*(8), 845–856. https://doi.org/10.1097/00005650-199608000-00011
Jackson, L. E. (1993). Understanding, eliciting and negotiating clients' multicultural health beliefs. *The Nurse Practitioner*, *18*(4), 30–43.
Jamet, D. (2018). The neological functions of disease euphemisms in English and French: Verbal hygiene or speech pathology? *Lexis, Journal in English Lexicology*, *12*. https://doi.org/10.4000/lexis.2397
Ji, M., Sørensen, K., & Bouillon, P. (2020). User-oriented healthcare translation and communication. In M. Ji & S. Laviosa (Eds.), *The Oxford handbook of translation and social practices* (p. 23). Oxford: Oxford University Press. https://archive-ouverte.unige.ch/unige:136727
Kagawa-Singer, M., & Kassim-Lakha, S. (2003). A strategy to reduce cross-cultural miscommunication and increase the likelihood of improving health outcomes. *Academic Medicine*, *78*(6), 577–587. https://doi.org/10.1097
Keifenheim, K. E., Teufel, M., Ip, J., Speiser, N., Leehr, E. J., Zipfel, S., & Herrmann-Werner, A. (2015). Teaching history taking to medical students: A systematic review. *BMC Medical Education*, *15*, 159. https://doi.org/10.1186/s12909-015-0443-x
Kissane, D. W., Bultz, D. B., Butow, P. N., Bylund, C. L., Noble, S., & Wilkinson, S. (2017). *Oxford textbook of communication in oncology and palliative care*. Oxford: Oxford University Press.
Latifnejad Roudsari, R., Javadnoori, M., Hasanpour, M., Hazavehei, S. M., & Taghipour, A. (2013). Socio-cultural challenges to sexual health education for female adolescents in Iran. *Iranian Journal of Reproductive Medicine*, *11*(2), 101–110.
Levin, H., Howard, G., & Peter, G. (1994). The effects of lexical formality and accent on trait attributions. *Language and Communication*, *14*(3), 265–274.
Linfoot-Ham, K. (2005). The linguistics of euphemism: A diachronic study of euphemism formation. *Journal of Language and Linguistics*, *4*(2), 227–263.
Maniya, O., & McGreevy, J. (2020). Managing emergency department risk through communication and documentation. *Emergency Medicine Clinics*, *38*(2). https://doi.org/10.1016/j.emc.2020.01.007

Mead, N., & Bower, P. (2002). Patient-centred consultations and outcomes in primary care: A review of the literature. *Patient Education and Counseling, 48*, 51–61. doi: 10.1016/s0738-3991(02)00099-x

McIntosh, P. (1989). White privilege: Unpacking the invisible knapsack. *Peace and Freedom*, 10–12.

MirzaiiNajmabadi, K., Karimi, L., & Ebadi, A. (2019). Exploring the barriers to sexual and reproductive health education for men in Iran: A qualitative study. *Iranian Journal of Nursing Midwifery Research, 24*(3), 179–186. https://doi.org/10.4103/ijnmr.IJNMR_132_18

Mosavi, S. A., Babazadeh, R., Najmabadi, K. M., & Shariati, M. (2014). Assessing Iranian adolescent girls' needs for sexual and reproductive health information. *The Journal of Adolescent Health: Official Publication of the Society for Adolescent Medicine, 55*(1), 107–113. https://doi.org/10.1016/j.jadohealth.2013.11.029

Mutal, J. D., Bouillon, P., Gerlach, J., Estrella, P., & Spechbach, H. (2019). Monolingual backtranslation in a medical speech translation system for diagnostic interviews: A NMT approach. In M. Forcada, A. Way, J. Tinsley, D. Shterionov, C. Rico, & F. Gaspari (Eds.), *Proceedings of machine translation summit XVII volume 2: Translator, project and user tracks* (pp. 169–203). European Association for Machine Translation. www.aclweb.org/anthology/W19-67.pdf

Napier, D., Depledge, M., Knipper, M., Lovell, R., Ponarin, E., Sanabria, E., & Thomas, F. (2017). Culture matters: Using a cultural contexts of health approach to enhance policy making. *Cultural Contexts of Health and Well-Being, No. 1.* World Health Organization, Regional Office for Europe.

Pitt, M. B., & Hendrickson, M. A. (2020). Eradicating jargon-oblivion-A proposed classification system of medical jargon. *Journal of General Internal Medicine, 35*(6), 1861–1864. https://doi.org/10.1007/s11606-019-05526-1

Priebe, S., Sandhu, S., Dias, S., Gaddini, A., Greacen, T., Ioannidis, E., Kluge, U., Krasnik, A., Lamkaddem, M., Lorant, V., Riera, R. P., Sarvary, A., Soares, J. J., Stankunas, M., Strassmayr, C., Wahlbeck, K., Welbel, M., & Bogic, M. (2011). Good practice in health care for migrants: Views and experiences of care professionals in 16 European countries. *BMC Public Health, 11*, 187. https://doi.org/10.1186/1471-2458-11-187

Pun, J. K., Matthiessen, C. M., Murray, K. A., & Slade, D. (2015). Factors affecting communication in emergency departments: Doctors and nurses' perceptions of communication in a trilingual ED in Hong Kong. *International Journal of Emergency Medicine, 8*(1), 48. https://doi.org/10.1186/s12245-015-0095-y

Qanbar, N. (2011). A sociolinguistic study of the linguistic taboos in the Yemeni society. *Modern Journal of Applied Linguistics, 3*(2), 86–104.

Rabab'ah, G., & Al-Qarni, A. (2012). Euphemism in Saudi Arabic and British English. *Journal of Pragmatics, 44*, 730–743. https://doi.org/10.1016/j.pragma.2012.02.008

Radulovic, M. (2016). Euphemisms through time: The rhetorical power of palliation. *Facta Universitatis, 14*(2), 173–187. doi: 10.22190/FULL1602173R

Randhawa, G., Ferreyra, M., Ahmed, R., Ezzat, O., & Pottie, K. (2013). Using machine translation in clinical practice. *Canadian Family Physician, 59*(4), 382–383.

Rathert, C., Wyrwich, M. D., & Boren, S. A. (2013). Patient-centered care and outcomes: A systematic review of the literature. *Medical Care Research and Review: MCRR, 70*(4), 351–379. https://doi.org/10.1177/1077558712465774

Rayner, E., Armando, A., Bouillon, P., Ebling, S., Gerlach, J., Halimi Mallem, I. S., & Tsourakis, N. (2016). Helping domain experts build phrasal speech translation systems. In J. F. Quesada, F. J. Martin Mateos, & T. Lopez-Soto (Eds.), *Future and emergent trends in language technology* (pp. 41–52). Switzerland: Springer. https://archive-ouverte.unige.ch/unige:77666

Rayner, E., Gerlach, J., Bouillon, P., Tsourakis, N., & Spechbach, H. (2018). Handling ellipsis in a spoken medical phraselator. In T. Dutoit, C. Martín-Vide, & G. Pironkov (Eds.), *Statistical language and speech processing: SLSP 2018* (pp. 140–152). Switzerland: Springer. https://archive-ouverte.unige.ch/unige:110589

Rodriguez, H., Rogers, W., Marshall, R., & Safran, D. (2007). Multidisciplinary primary care teams: Effects on the quality of clinician-patient interactions and organizational features of care. *Medical Care, 45*, 19–27. doi: 10.1097/01.mlr.0000241041.53804.29

Rowland, D. L. (2020). Culture and practice: Identifying the issues. In D. L. Rowland & E. A. Jannini (Eds.), *Cultural differences and the practice of sexual medicine* (pp. 3–21). Switzerland: Springer.

Santana, M., Manalili, K., Jolley, R., Zelinsky, S., Quan, H., & Lu, M. (2018). How to practice person-centred care: A conceptual framework. *Health Expectations, 21*(2), 429–440. https://doi.org/10.1111/hex.12640

Serrant-Green, L. (2005). Breaking traditions: Sexual health and ethnicity in nursing research: A literature review. *Journal of Advanced Nursing, 51*(5), 511–519. https://doi.org/10.1111/j.1365-2648.2005.03518.x

Slade, D., Manidis, M., McGregor, J., Scheeres, H., Chandler, E., Stein-Parbury, J., Dunston, R., Herke, M., & Matthiessen, C. M. I. M. (2015). *Communicating in hospital emergency departments*. Berlin: Springer. https://doi.org/10.1007/978-3-662-46021_4

Sontag, S. (1978). *Illness as metaphor and AIDS and Its Metaphors*. New York: Farrar, Straus and Giroux.

Spechbach, H., Gerlach, J., Mazouri Karker, S., Tsourakis, N., Combescure, C., & Bouillon, P. (2019). A speech-enabled fixed-phrase translator for emergency settings: Crossover study. *JMIR Medical Informatics, 7*(2), e13167. https://doi.org/10.2196/13167

Stewart, M. (2005). I'm just going to wash you down: Sanitizing the vaginal examination. *Journal of Advanced Nursing, 51*(6), 587–594. https://doi.org/10.1111/j.1365-2648.2005.03543.x

Swift, J. A., Choi, E., Puhl, R. M., & Glazebrook, C. (2013). Talking about obesity with clients: Preferred terms and communication styles of U.K. pre-registration dieticians, doctors, and nurses. *Patient Education and Counseling, 91*(2), 186–191. https://doi.org/10.1016/j.pec.2012.12.008

Tacheva, V. (2013). Communication: The master key to the patient's heart. *JAHR: European Journal of Bioethics, 4*(7), 601–620.

Tailor, A., & Ogden, J. (2009). Avoiding the term "obesity": An experimental study of the impact of doctors' language on patients' beliefs. *Patient Education and Counseling*, *76*(2), 260–264. https://doi.org/10.1016/j.pec.2008.12.016

Tamimi Sa'd, S. (2017). A sociolinguistic analysis of taboos and euphemisms in an Arab community in Iran. *Dialectologia*, *18*, 107–127.

Tayler, M., & Ogden, J. (2005). Doctors' use of euphemisms and their impact on patients' beliefs about health: An experimental study of heart failure. *Patient Education and Counseling*, *57*(3), 321–326. https://doi.org/10.1016/j.pec.2004.09.001

Taylor, R. M., Crichton, N., Moult, B., & Gibson, F. (2015). A prospective observational study of machine translation software to overcome the challenge of including ethnic diversity in healthcare research. *Nursing Open*, *2*(1), 14–23. https://doi.org/10.1002/nop2.13

Traumer, L., Jacobsen, M. H., & Laursen, B. S. (2019). Patients' experiences of sexuality as a taboo subject in the Danish healthcare system: A qualitative interview study. *Scandinavian Journal of Caring Sciences*, *33*(1), 57–66. https://doi.org/10.1111/scs.12600

van Wieringen, J. C., Harmsen, J. A., & Bruijnzeels, M. A. (2002). Intercultural communication in general practice. *European Journal of Public Health*, *12*(1), 63–68. https://doi.org/10.1093/eurpub/12.1.63

Warren, B. (1992). What euphemisms tell us about the interpretation of words. *Studia Linguistica*, *46*(2), 128–182.

Weijts, W., Houtkoop, H., & Mullen, P. (1993). Talking delicacy: Speaking about sexuality during gynaecological consultations. *Sociology of Health & Illness*, *15*(3), 295–314.

2 MDA analysis of translated and non-translated parliamentary discourse

María Calzada-Pérez and María del Mar Sánchez Ramos

1 Introduction

Corpus-based translation studies (CTS) are inextricably linked to the name of Mona Baker. It was Baker who, among other things, officially declared the existence of this area of study in a seminal paper published in 1993, in which she foresaw:

> a turning point in the history of the discipline. I would like to argue that this turning point will come as a direct consequence of access to large corpora of both original and translated texts, and the development of specific methods and tools for interrogating such corpora in ways which are appropriate to the needs of translation scholars.
>
> (Baker, 1993, p. 235)

Her words anticipated a frantic proliferation of translation-related corpora, which have hitherto undoubtedly enriched translation studies (TS) by providing "new ways of looking at translation" (Kenny, 1998, p. 53). In particular (and among other things), this has increased the "search for patterns that identify translation qua translation" (Laviosa, 2011, p. 18) as part of the identification of what are known as translation universals (Mauranen & Kujamäki, 2004). This has also been furthered in the examination of translator style (Saldanha, 2011).

With almost 30 years since the publication of Baker's (1993) paper, we can certainly argue that CTS has come of age. We can equally advocate that the time has come to pause for reflection. We are not alone in this view. In a particularly illuminating exercise of self-reflexivity, De Sutter and Lefer (2020) start pondering. They look back into CTS (reasonably mature) history and identify four main problems: a neglect of the notion of similarity and an excessive emphasis on difference; the construction of an underdeveloped theoretical framework that does not follow the stages of

DOI: 10.4324/9781003102694-2

solid, empirical research; the monofactorial nature of research "in which the distribution of a linguistic phenomenon is investigated with reference to one explanatory factor" (De Sutter & Lefer, 2020, p. 5); and the auto-isolation of studies. All of these problems, in their view, result in a reductionist approach that impacts the reliability of the framework, putting into jeopardy its abundant results so far.

De Sutter and Lefer (2020, p. 6) also look ahead and present us with "a new, updated research agenda" in which CTS is to have the following attributes. It is to be multifactorial, embracing the fact that "understanding translation implies understanding its multidimensional structure, and hence multifactorial research designs are essential". Moreover, it is to be interdisciplinary, and it is to be related to other forms of communication with which it shares processes and products. Finally, it is to be multimethodological; hence, new methods are to be explored for progress to occur.

The present chapter largely shares De Sutter and Lefer's (2020) declaration of intentions and aims at contributing to the new agenda of these scholars. More specifically, we tentatively intend to enhance CTS's multifactorial and multimethodological nature through an exploration of Biber's (1988) interdisciplinary multidimensional analysis (MDA). In building on a multifactorial design, MDA is a clearly underrepresented method in TS. The interdisciplinary nature of its origins (MDA stems from discourse analysis, corpus linguistics, computer studies, and statistics) fights reductionism and exacerbates the complexity of its theoretical basis while adding an empirical slant to its methodology.

In what follows, we have an exploratory go at an MDA study of parliamentary translated and non-translated discourse in English drawing on 2005 language samples from the *European Comparable and Parallel Corpus Archive of European Parliamentary Discourse* (ECPC). Exploring the nature of parliamentary discourse makes sense for its own merits. Parliaments are institutions of the utmost importance to global governance. A wide array of topics (of often great importance for the everyday man and woman) are discussed within its chambers. An ample variety of people (members of parliament, mostly) and styles (informed by ideologies) are confronted and used to pursue similar and dissimilar strategic goals. In the same way, parliaments are a democratic representation of society at large, and parliamentary production is a relatively controlled sample of communication in general. Parliamentary subcorpora may be seen, therefore, to safeguard a form of the representativity that is always so fundamental to Biber's work. In other words, with its own specifics, of course (parliamentary speech is a genre on its own, after all), one could argue that examining interventions from parliaments is a possible gateway to measuring the state of our societies. Nevertheless, our interest in the ECPC subcorpora here transcends the parliamentary setting and enters the linguistic arena. European parliamentary houses are impeccably comparable settings for delving into different varieties of translated and non-translated Englishes (such as those from the European Parliament, EP, and the House of Commons, HC). There are other situations of a similar (yet in some respects utterly dissimilar) form (for example, the academic genres analysed by Conrad, 2001). However, the specific cases of the EP (with its translated and non-translated yet possibly "contaminated" Euro-jargon English; for Euro-jargon, see, for instance, Koskinen, 2008, p. 43) and HC (with its relatively independent "pristine" production of "proper" English) offer a plausible scenario for delving into the impact of (translational) contexts on language varieties.

It is important to reinforce that our main motivations through this piece of research are exploratory in nature and humble in their aspirations. However, we see exploration as a necessary inductive (bottom-up) step to establishing solid grounds for upcoming examinations. Our exploration here adopts the following structure. The introduction presented in section 1 is followed in section 2 by a brief contextualization of Biber's (1988) MDA with some of its main principles and working stages. Section 3 introduces the ECPC subcorpora, upon which the study is performed together with the main methodological stages used. Section 4 describes the analysis and discusses the results. The chapter ends with concluding remarks.

2 Brief account of Biber's (1988) multidimensional analysis and its application within TS

2.1 Biber's (1988) multidimensional analysis

One of the ways in which De Sutter and Lefer's (2020) new agenda for empirical translation studies may be pursued is by applying (and ultimately adopting) Biber's (1988) multidimensional analysis (MDA). According to Biber (2014), MDA was born during the 1980s under the influence of two of his mentors at the University of South California: Ed Purcell (who taught him "both statistical analysis as well as advanced computer programming skills"; Biber, 2014, p. 30) and Ed Finegan (his dissertation chair, described by Biber as "central to my development as a corpus linguist, and as a researcher and writer in general"; Biber, 2014, p. 30). Additionally, Biber found inspiration from works by Ervin-Tripp, Firth, Halliday, and Hymes (among others), who noted the importance of correlation for the study of language (Biber, 2019, p. 12). He also drew on research advocating the need for empirical approaches to register variation, such as those presented by Chafe (1982) and Longacre (1976) (cited in Biber, 2019, p. 12). He was especially seduced by Carroll's (1960; cited in Biber, 2019, p. 12) visionary study of "vectors of prose style", employing a statistical analysis of linguistic co-occurrence patterns. That the development of MDA mobilized this ample gamut of interdisciplinary knowledge and skills gives a sense of how very polyhedric and demanding it is.

In brief, MDA is an approach to the study of (monolingual and multilingual) language that ultimately targets "texts, registers, and text types, rather than . . . individual linguistic constructions" (Biber, 1995b, p. 343). Its main ingredients are (1) a corpus-based platform; (2) computational techniques for the automatic identification and disambiguation of linguistic features; (3) multivariate statistics to identify co-occurrence patterns (factors) and relations among texts; and (4) a methodological synthesis of (quantitative) techniques and (qualitative) functional methods, according to which statistical data are interpreted in functional terms. In sum, MDA works under the assumption that:

> strong co-occurrence patterns of linguistic features mark underlying functional dimensions. Features do not randomly occur, then it is reasonable to look for an underlying functional influence that encourages their use. In this way, these functions are not posited on an a priori basis; rather they are required to account for the observed co-occurrence patterns among linguistic features.
>
> (Biber, 1988, p. 13)

Most importantly, and according to Biber (1988, p. 20), MDA takes the researcher to a "multi-dimensional space". Here, analysts do not content themselves with examining data from a one-dimensional perspective by focusing, for example, on a particular language feature within a more or less ample gamut of contexts or, vice versa, by studying multiple features as used in a specific language context/text. Neither is research limited to a two-dimensional prism, whereby two kinds of linguistic items are under scrutiny in the same (more or less varied) number of contexts or according to which a large number of features are dissected within two different settings of language use. Instead, MDA analysts aim at the examination of a large/multiple number of linguistic features in a (more or less wide) multiple range of contexts. Multiplicity is required because, as Biber (1995b, p. 343) argues, "[N]o single linguistic parameter is adequate in itself to capture the range of similarities and differences among spoken and written registers". Hence, we have the multidimensional label.

Biber's MDA departs from real data belonging to different (oral and written) genres and moves upwards in four stages: (1) the identification of variables (i.e., language features) to be examined; (2) the extraction of correlations/factors from variables; (3) the functional interpretation of factors as dimensions; and (4) an overall reflection on relations. The accomplishment of all four stages is what it is called a "Full multidimensional analysis" (Brezina, 2018, p. 161).

In stage 1, analysts must select a list of linguistic features (such as past tense and time adverbials or nominalizations, to name a few for the purposes of illustration) upon which the analysis will be performed. In different implementations of MDA, this list ranges from 40 to 190 items. For example, Biber's (1988) seminal research works with 67 features (the same ones we use in our study here; for the full list, see Appendix II in Biber, 1988, pp. 221–245). His prior PhD dissertation (Biber, 1984) covers 42 variables. Recent applications of the MDA model have increased this span, with Xiao's (2009) 141 items and Berber-Sardinha et al. (2014) 190 features.

In stage 2, statistical correlations of the chosen linguistic features are extracted from large pools of corpora (Biber's, 1988 corpora contained 481 oral and written text samples from 21 different genres). Correlation groupings are known as factors and are identified through the multivariate statistical technique of factor analysis described by Brezina (2018, p. 164) as follows:

> a complex mathematical procedure that reduces a large number of linguistic variables to a small number of factors, each combining multiple linguistic variables. This is done by considering correlations between variables . . .; those that correlate – both positively and negatively – are considered components of the same factor because they have a connection. Positive correlations mean that the variables show the same pattern of occurrence in the data, while negative correlation indicates complementary distribution, that is, if one variable appears with a high frequency the other appears infrequently and vice versa.

In stage 3, MDA pursues connections between factors and language-related situations through the notion of functions. Since all linguistic items are used for a purpose, it is precisely the interpretative analysis of this purpose that serves to make qualitative sense of the statistical data. It is at this stage that correlations/factors become "dimensions":

> Dimensions represent distinct groupings of linguistic features that have been empirically determined to co-occur with significant frequencies in texts. It is important to note that the co-occurring patterns underlying dimensions are identified quantitatively (by statistical factor analysis) and not on any a priori basis. Dimensions are subsequently interpreted in terms of the communicative functions shared by the co-occurring features. Interpretative labels are posited for each dimension.
> (Biber, 1995b, p. 344)

Biber (1988, chapter 6) identifies six dimensions through which oral and written genres are examined. These six dimensions are among Biber's most important research findings and constitute six different perspectives from which to attempt to produce functional interpretations of the (sub)corpora under study. Due to space constraints, these six dimensions are listed here. Further details about them will be provided as part of our analysis on a need basis. They are:

Dimension 1: "Informational versus Involved Production"
Dimension 2: "Narrative versus Non-narrative Concerns"
Dimension 3: "Explicit versus Situation-Dependent Reference"
Dimension 4: "Overt Expression of Persuasion"
Dimension 5: "Abstract versus Non-Abstract Information"
Dimension 6: "Online Informational Elaboration"

Finally, in stage 4, MDA aims at establishing relations between and among texts (within registers or configurations) and between and among registers (within the linguistic production of speakers/writers or institutions). Relations between and among dimensions may also be scrutinised by MDA, making the approach especially multifaceted.

In sum, Biber's (1988) MDA is a mixed-method research framework that combines quantitative and qualitative components. In addition, it is precisely the latter that, according to Friginal and Hardy (2019, p. 146), constitutes its "real purpose", as they note:

> To summarize, although it may seem driven by frequency counts, z-scores, and complex statistics, MD Analysis does not exist in a purely quantitative paradigm. Without qualitative interpretation, there is little meaning to the findings of a linguistic FA.
> (Friginal & Hardy, 2019, p. 147)

One qualitative MDA approach involves drawing a comparison to Biber's (1988) original dimensions rather than performing a full MDA. When choosing to do so, researchers skip Stages 1–3 (previously noted) and concentrate on Stage 4 by comparing their results to Biber's material. Relying on Biber's dimensions for qualitative interpretation makes sense since they derive from six factors that "have strong factorial structures, and the features grouped on each factor are functionally coherent and can be readily interpreted on the basis of prior microscopic research" (Biber, 1988, p. 115). This is precisely what we do in section 5. We believe that Biber's well-established dimensions provide a strong interpretative starting point that can inform forthcoming full MDA work, in which we will propose our own factors and dimensions in a more independent manner.

The quantification of real data and their interpretation according to functions, underlying dimensions, and relations make MDA "as much as an art as it is a science . . . it requires technical knowledge of the structure of the language, but it also demands skill, inspiration, and imagination" (Biber, 2014, p. xvi). It is precisely this twofold technical-inspirational/imaginative requirement that makes MDA particularly demanding for researchers, especially in computational and statistical terms.

However, despite its difficulties, MDA has gradually evolved over time with incipient steps represented by Biber (1984) as a direct precursor to the canonical presentation of the MDA model in Biber (1988). Further developments followed suit, especially during the 1990s and beyond. These developments have included, among others, (a) contrastive analyses of different languages (Biber, 1995a); (b) collaborations between Biber himself and PhD students applying MDA to other languages (Besnier, 1988; Biber & Hared, 1992; Kim & Biber, 1994) and (c) diachronic studies describing the evolution of registers (Biber & Finegan, 1992). MDA has transcended Biber's direct area of influence, and scholars from all over the world have used it to explore a large number of research interests, as Berber-Sardinha and Veirano-Pinto (2014, 2019) testify. That a limited yet reasonable number of research items have been produced within the MDA constellation shows how "powerful" (Brezina, 2018, p. 149) and "reliable" (Nini, 2019, pp. 77–82) MDA is considered to be.

2.2 Multidimensional analysis and translation

Multivariate approaches (such as MDA) have also entered the realm of TS. Admittedly, this has occurred at a slow and hesitant pace, in part due to the difficult technical-inspirational/imaginative requirements mentioned earlier. Nevertheless, with De Sutter and Lefer (2020, p. 1), a handful of other researchers have already approached translation "as an inherently multidimensional linguistic activity and product" (De Sutter & Lefer, 2020, p. 1). In TS, MDA-impregnated projects date at least as far back as Xiao (2010), which focuses on original and translated Chinese within the larger body of translation universals.

Other scholars such as Delaere and De Sutter (2017), Hu et al. (2016), Ji (2017), Kruger (2019), and Kruger and Van Rooy (2016) serve as good examples of how multivariate statistics help go beyond confusing, potentially reductionist, and often unsubstantiated discussions by opening TS's investigative lens for research. For example, Hu et al. (2016) show that, unlike prior research, translation universals are not to be taken for granted and that empirical translation studies are to proceed from the bottom to the top. Ji (2017) carries out a multifactorial study of universals where different genres (of translated and non-translated production) are considered at once and where shifts and similarities happen not only locally (among particular features) but also and mainly globally (at the level of genres). Delaere and Sutter (2017), Kruger (2019), and Kruger and Van Rooy (2016) test a larger range of potential causes of the nature of translational texts (such as the bilingual activation mode, the transference of a pre-existing text, cognitive complexity, the SL transfer hypothesis, and above all, pragmatic risk aversion). Kruger and Van Rooy (2016) also bring translation studies to a more open space where they escape autoisolation to establish contact with other forms of "constrained communication" (such as that of the non-native production of English). Finally, De Sutter and Lefer (2020) and especially Kruger (2019) show how very far multivariate studies take us in the empirical examination of previously analysed translational phenomena (such as the implicit/explicit use of "that" with verbs such as "say" or "tell" in translated and non-translated texts). In summary, as a field, TS is problematised to a rather more complex and comprehensive extent when explored with approaches such as MDA.

Studies such as these show that translation is certainly a legitimate (and fruitful) object of study for multidimensional approaches. This is only logical, since MDA's application gravitates around "the situation", Biber's (1988, chapter 2) pivotal notion to justify the existence of language varieties (attending to particular needs or functions) upon which MDA can be performed. Biber (1988) devotes a large part of chapter 2 to the definition of "the situation", whose components are grounded on Brown and Fraser (1979) and Hymes (1974) (cited in Biber, 1988). Taking these studies as a starting point, Biber (1988) names its main components, which in our view are highly applicable to the case of translation. The first component of all situations is participants' roles and characteristics. Similar to other situations, there is no doubt that translations have addressors, addressees, and audiences; furthermore, a special type of participant is involved in the translation process, which makes translating unique: the translator or mediator. The second component of such situations pertains to the relations among participants. As in other situations before, during and after translation, participants establish a number of connections (i.e., social, status, or personal relations) with one another. The ample work by Lefevere is seminal in the analysis of, in particular, social and status relations within the translation world. The third collection of situational components includes the setting (where and when communication takes place), topic (what the message is about), and purpose ("outcomes that participants hope for, expect, or intend from the communicative event"; Biber, 1988, p. 32). These three components merge into what Biber (1988) labels "the scene". There is a translational scene defined as much as any other "constrained" (De Sutter &

Lefer, 2020; Kruger & Van Rooy, 2016) communicative scene. Biber (1988) concludes his examination of situations with a proposal of three pivotal components that are central to the translation process: social evaluation (see sociological approaches in TS); participants' relations to the text – as Munday (2012) shows in his adaptation of Martin and White's (2005) work to translation – and the channel, which through translation give rise at least two subtypes of communication: written translation and oral interpretation.

Overall, translations are the result of an urge to communicate specific messages in a particular situation. This is Biber's starting point for deploying MDA procedures and protocols. Consequently, for all the reasons mentioned in this section, we apply MDA to translation in what we consider is a rather innovative way, with the intention of contributing to strengthening the discipline.

3 Methodology

The study described here is an exploratory attempt to perform an MDA on a set of (translated and non-translated) corpora of parliamentary speech in English.

The corpora used for the present analysis belong to the *European Comparable and Parallel Corpus Archive of Parliamentary Discourse* (ECPC). Compiled at Universitat Jaume I (Castellón, Spain), the archive contains (2005–2014) translated and original speeches and writings from (i) the EP in (original and translated) English and Spanish; (ii) the UK House of Commons (HC); and (iii) the Spanish *Congreso de los Diputados* (CD). The specific subcorpora selected for this research contain material in English as follows:

EP_EN_ST_05: Original speeches and written interventions in English from 2005 (870,262 tokens) as published in the *Official Journal of the European Union* (OJEU). This corpus has a standardised type/token ratio (STTR) of 41.20 and a standard deviation (SD) of 58.53. Mean of words per sentence: 22.40.

EP_EN_TT_05: Translated speeches and written interventions into English from 2005 (2,208,677 tokens) as published in the *Official Journal of the European Union* (OJEU). This corpus has a standardised type/token ratio (STTR) of 41.28 and a standard deviation (SD) of 58.69. Mean of words per sentence: 26.27.

HC_05: British MPs' speeches and written interventions from 2005 (7,892,405 tokens) as published in *Hansard*. This corpus has an STTR of 39.20 and an SD of 60.77. Mean of words per sentence: 19.67.

Although we could have used the whole ECPC archive for our study, we opted for a one-year (2005) set of subcorpora for a variety of reasons. First, a one-year set of subcorpora seems to be a reasonably large yet manageable amount of linguistic production (totalling 10,971,344 tokens). We see this decision as a compromise between large and small sizes, which helps us with MDA's technical features (too small a corpus may not yield statistically reliable data) while allowing us to control the imaginative requirement as well (too large a corpus will cause researchers to lose sight of details, which often matter for inspirational purposes). Additionally, we conceive of this research as exploratory in nature. We depart with no preconceptions and set off to merely consider the effectiveness of potential synergies between MDA and TS. A set of speeches given in one year seems to be a logical departing point for an exploratory voyage. Finally, our specific focus on 2005 is partly random (2005 is as good or bad as any other year and represents the first full year of speech data from the ECPC Archive) and partly motivated by the fact that it was an eventful year for the EU in which the European Constitution was finally rejected with considerable opposition from the United Kingdom, among others. This frantic activity regarding the Constitution is bound to be reflected by (translated and non-translated) English excerpts of material from the EP and House of Commons. It is then, a priori, a good period for exploring similarities and differences.

Hence, in this exploratory study, our departing research questions are kept at a very general (humble, as stated earlier) level and may be phrased in the following manner:

- Can MDA's empirical methodology shed light on the similarities and differences between (translated and non-translated) language in three different types of situations: (a) when original speakers use English for communication at the European Parliament; (b) when translators produce an English version of non-English interventions; and (c) when members of Parliament (MPs) express themselves at the House of Commons? Would it be possible to locate language production in Biberian dimensions and make functional sense of the results?
- Can a TS perspective illuminate and enrich MDA's (largely though not exclusively) monolingual studies?

To answer these questions, drawing mainly on Biber (1988) and reviews by Brezina (2018) and Friginal and Hardy (2019), we focus on the interpretative aspect of Biber's framework and proceed with an analysis involving a comparison to Biber's (1988) MDA results. In future research, we intend to conduct a full quantitative and qualitative study and pursue a full MDA of our corpora.

The present study developed over five stages. In Stage 1, we preprocessed our XML ECPC Archive to revert it to plain TXT format. Each of the

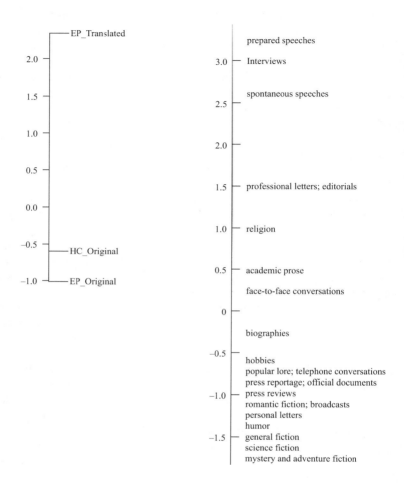

Figure 2.1 Example of LSTO results

subcorpora under study includes files containing one-day speeches that have been stripped of all ECPC metadata. With this preprocessing, we could then proceed to Stage 2 and use Nini's MAT (Nini, 2014, 2019). In brief, MAT is a computer programme that (a) produces grammatically annotated versions of TXT (sub)corpora under study using Biber's (1988) 67 linguistic features and (b) generates relative frequencies of these features per hundred words (among other things). Stage 3 required the use of Brezina's Lancaster Stats Tool Online (LSTO). This is a website where MAT-generated frequencies are inserted to produce graphs of researchers' results alongside Biber's six dimensions, as shown in Figure 2.1. Note that, if required, the LSTO may also generate numerical and graphical data to perform a full MDA study (which will be useful in forthcoming studies). Stage 4 involved a qualitative analysis of LSTO-produced graphs. In response to the questions posed previously, we aimed to present plausible explanations for ECPC phenomena based on Biber's (1988) dimensions and to complement Biber's framework with ECPC results. In Stage 5, we drew some global conclusions on (original and translated) parliamentary communication from the independently produced examinations of each of Biber's dimensions performed in the previous stage.

4 Analysis and results

As mentioned earlier, the present chapter departs from Biber's MDA in Stage 4 and involves a comparison of his 1988 results to those of EP_EN_ST_05, EP_EN_TT_05, and HC_05. Due to space constraints, we limit the presentation of results to Biber's (1988) dimensions 1, 2, and 6, which are the most prominent for our subcorpora. Hence, the analysis that follows goes through each of these three dimensions. For each dimension, we first present a summary of Biber's interpretation and then examine and exploit its potential to explain our data, which may also contribute to Biber's framework. Before proceeding further, it seems fitting to recall that each dimension reflects a viewpoint from which data may be interpreted.

4.1 Dimension 1

Biber's (1988, p. 107) dimension 1 measures "Informational versus Involved Production". It is a continuum with "high informational density and exact informational content" in the lower end and "affective, interactional, and generalised content" at the top. Thus, texts and registers with low scores on this dimension (e.g., biographies, press reviews, academic prose, press reports, and official documents) are highly informative and lexically precise. They tend to be texts and registers that are less influenced by time/place constraints and that have "careful editing possibilities, enabling precision in lexical choice and an integrated textual structure" (Biber, 1988, p. 107). By contrast, texts and registers with high scores here (e.g., telephone and face-to-face conversations, personal letters, spontaneous speeches, and interviews) occur under circumstances of real-time production and can be seen as "constrained" language (De Sutter & Lefer, 2020; Kruger & Van Rooy,

2016) heavily subjected to communicative settings. Editing is not normally possible at this end, and information is presented in a fragmented, more affective manner. In between the top and bottom poles of the dimension are texts and registers with mixed features of informational and involved forms (e.g., romantic fiction, prepared speeches, mystery and adventure fiction, general fiction, professional letters, and broadcasts). Figure 2.2 captures Biber's dimension 1.

Dimension 1 is built from a very long list of positive and negative correlations of features, making it convoluted to interpret. High scores of positive correlation features especially point to the involved (top) end of the dimension. Among them, and for the sake of illustration, we can especially mention private verbs, THAT deletion, contractions, present tense verbs, etc. That is, all of these features appear together in a significant manner and help distribute texts and registers along an involved versus non-involved gradation. High scores of negatively correlated features point to the bottom, informative end of the dimension. Among them, there are nouns, word lengths, prepositions, type/token ratios, etc. Again, all features with negative scores significantly correlate and contribute to distinguishing between more or less informative texts and registers.[1]

Dimension 1 is one of the two fundamental dimensions included in Biber's (1988) study (the other being dimension 2, discussed later). Biber (1988) presents solid significance values (F-value = 119.9 and p-value < .0001) and a high Pearson's correlation factor (r^2 = 84.3%). According to Biber (1988, p. 126): "The RxR value indicates the percentage of variation in the dimension scores of texts that can be accounted for by knowing the genre category of the text". In other words, an r^2 of 84.3% means that the dimension 1 parameter accounts for 84.3% of the distribution of the continuum depicted in Figure 2.2. This dimension is then so fundamental that it even qualifies as a candidate "for universal parameters of register variation" (Berber-Sardinha & Veirano-Pinto, 2014, p. xxxiii), which implies that it is supposed to be a determining parameter in distinguishing between and among all (and any) kinds of texts/registers.

However, for our ECPC (original and translated) subcorpora, dimension 1 is largely unimportant (see Figure 2.3).

Its r^2 is a mere 2.8%, meaning that it has a dimension explanatory power of just 2.8%. From a different perspective, the figure shows that over 97% of the variation is here explained by factors other than dimension 1. Additionally, these results, though potentially significant in the human science field (F = 3.6; p < 0.05), are not of the most stringent (e.g., p < 0.01 or below). Among others, this may suggest that for this dimension to be more stable, more data may be required. Consequently, regarding dimension 1, the results for the ECPC subcorpora are to be taken with great caution. At any rate, our results may cast doubt over dimension 1 as a strong candidate

Parliamentary discourse 39

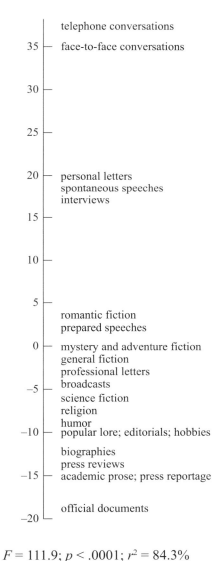

$F = 111.9; p < .0001; r^2 = 84.3\%$

Figure 2.2 Biber's dimension 1

for universal variation. Even if it has been regarded as a pivotal parameter for distinguishing between and among all texts (it has, after all, some – a 2.8% – significant contributing role in text/register allocation along the dimension), it must be acknowledged that it may have a much lesser impact

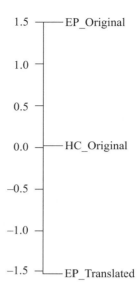

$F = 3.6; p = 0.02781206, r^2 = 2.8\%$

Figure 2.3 ECPC (original and translated) subcorpora's dimension 1

on results than what Biber's research indicates, depending of course on the kind of study performed.

Taking into consideration all the limitations of dimension 1, we can still say that some of these results are not, however, altogether inexplicable. If dimension 1 is related – among others and as Biber (1988, p. 107) emphasises above – to the possibility of text editing, it is only natural that there is little difference (−1.5 to 1.5 span of variation) between our HC, EP_EN_ST_05, and EP_EN_TT_05 speeches, since all of these are taken from parliamentary proceedings, which are notoriously subjected to proofreading and editing. If editing occurs in all EP and HC cases, then this might partly explain why this parameter proves largely unable to capture similarities and differences among texts and registers. Along the same lines, it is also logical that translated speeches from the EP are more informational than their original EP counterparts since they undergo what may be seen as two rounds of editing: proofing and editing of the original text and then subsequent translation. It is more difficult to explain, however, why House of Commons speeches lie in the middle of our gradation, between translated and original production in EP English.

It is understandable that HC speeches are more exposed to real-time constraints than EP translated interventions due to the very nature of House of Commons debates (where most speakers, for example, are prompted to intervene by the Chair without prior warning and where no translation is required). However, it is not clear why HC speeches are less involved and more informational than original EP speeches. Paradoxically, the latter normally depend on previously scheduled participation by MEPs, who tend to read their interventions in almost all cases. Note again that at the House of Commons, the Chair asks MPs to participate on the spot, and they have very little time to react to the call, adding an element of pressure and improvisation to speech delivery.

Another surprising result is that although the ECPC data have a relatively similar span to that of Biber's prepared speeches (with a score of 2.2), it is remarkably far from his location of spontaneous speeches (with a score of 18.2). The prepared and spontaneous speeches examined by Biber were compiled as part of the 1960s London-Lund corpus. There, prepared speeches include as subgenres: sermons, university lectures, cases made in court, political speeches, and popular lectures. Spontaneous speeches include cases made in court, dinner speeches, radio essays, and speeches made in the House of Commons. Therefore, at first glance, the distance, especially between our HC speeches (at approximately 0.0 in the gradation) and Biber's spontaneous oration (at 18.2 in the gradation), seems baffling. However, we must remember that Biber's oration is directly transcribed by researchers from direct oral interventions while HC speeches are downloaded from already edited *Hansard* proceedings. While on the topic of where ECPC speeches stand along Biber's dimension 1, we should also briefly mention the interesting fact that the EP's original speeches come closer to Biber's (prepared) speeches.

Overall, some of our ECPC results (especially the location of EP translated texts along the continuum) may be (partly) explained by Biber's dimension 1. However, dimension 1 leaves more questions than answers regarding our data, which brings to mind its very low r^2 score. In turn, the ECPC corpora bring further food for thought on Biber's research. Of particular interest and from a translational viewpoint, we could do worse than consider translation as a special form of editing that could tamper with MDA results. Additionally, dimension 1 may well be a universal parameter for distinguishing between and among texts of a very different kind. When texts fulfil an array of similar goals in very different settings (with possibly very different overall aims), as is the case in our research (with EP and HC exchanges), this dimension may lose an enormous proportion of its explicatory capacity. Finally, the a priori most similar types found in ECPC and Biber's corpora and HC and Biber's (spontaneous) speeches are not necessarily closer in gradation. It is original EP speeches in English that resemble Biber's (prepared) speeches most closely.

4.2 Dimension 2

Biber's dimension 2 is "more straightforward than factor 1" (Biber, 1988, p. 108) and measures "Narrative versus Non-narrative Concerns". It thus reflects a continuum that differentiates between narrative discourse from other types of discourse. Texts and registers with high scores on this dimension (e.g., romantic fiction, mystery, science and general fiction, and adventure fiction) normally contain vivid imagery and constantly refer to the past, which frames the story being told. By contrast, texts and registers with low scores here (e.g., press reviews, telephone conversations, professional letters, academic prose, official documents, and broadcasts) tend to focus on the present, dealing "with more immediate matters" (Biber, 1988, p. 109). Between these is a range of genres from biographies and interviews to spontaneous and prepared speeches that display characteristics of both. Figure 2.4 captures Biber's dimension 2.

Dimension 2 is based on a much shorter list of positive and negative correlations of features than dimension 1, which partly explains why it is more straightforward. Positive correlation features include past tense verbs, third person pronouns, perfect aspect verbs, public verbs (introducing reported speech), synthetic negation, and present participial clauses. These features appear together in a significant manner to confer texts a narrative nature. Negative correlated features include present tense verbs, attributive adjectives, past participial deletions, and word length. Again, these features with negative scores significantly correlate to build a non-narrative (often official or professional) discourse.[2]

Together with dimension 1, dimension 2 is the other candidate as a universal parameter of variation. Biber (1988) presents solid significance values (F-value = 32.3 and p-value < .0001) and a high Pearson's correlation factor (r^2 = 60.8%). Hence, dimension 2 is highly significant and provides 60.8% of the explanation for Figure 2.4, becoming a very strong determining parameter underlying corpora.

For our ECPC subcorpora, dimension 2 is the most important determining parameter, and 2005's (original and translated) EP and HC parliamentary speeches are displaced on the gradation, as depicted in Figure 2.5.

This arrangement is extremely significant (F-value = 108.7 and p-value < 1.150504E-34) and highly explicative (r^2 = 46.6%) of ECPC corpora variation. Our results thus confirm that dimension 2 is a good candidate for grouping (and separating) texts such as those included in the ECPC subcorpora.

Parliamentary discourse 43

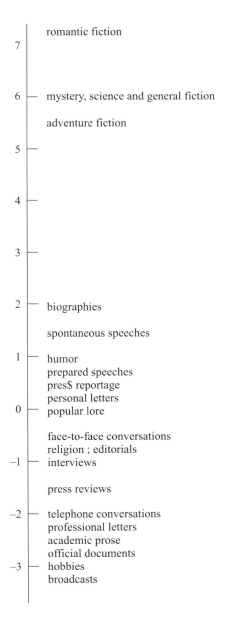

$F = 32.3; p < .0001; r^2 = 60.8\%$

Figure 2.4 Biber's dimension 2

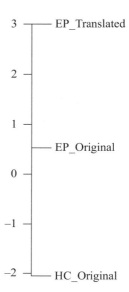

$F = 108.7; p = 1.150504\text{E}{-}34, r^2 = 46.6\%$

Figure 2.5 ECPC (original and translated) subcorpora's dimension 2

In our ECPC case, EP speeches in general (regardless of whether they are translated or original) are found to be more narrative than HC interventions. This result is absolutely logical due to the nature and structure of both EP and HC day sessions.

Briefly, and as explained in *The Plenary: a User's Guide* (revision 2019), the Plenary of the European Parliament currently meets four days a month (Monday to Thursday) in Strasbourg. Additional meetings are possible in Brussels. In the past (certainly in 2005, from which texts of our corpora were drawn), the EP normally met between four and six days a month. The Euro Chamber debates and votes on issues carefully included in agendas by the Conference of Presidents, which is composed of the Parliament's President and the leaders of political groups. At the Plenary, most speakers (rapporteurs, MEPs, representatives for the Council and Commission, etc.) are granted a short but fair amount of time (in advance) to advocate their positions in accordance with strict rules of procedures. There is a wide range of potential intervention profiles with their own assigned time slots. Short slots now happen, for example, under the "catch-the-eye" procedure, where MEPs attract the President's attention on a particular topic and, if granted permission, are allowed to speak for one minute. The catch-the-eye procedure did not exist in 2005, but one-minute interventions were possible at the time under a slightly different procedure. With this debating structure it comes as no surprise that EP debates excel in narrative concerns. On one hand, the Euro Chamber meets occasionally every month and must consequently look backwards (and forwards) to what happened before the Plenary (and what will happen afterwards). In fact, participants tend to narrate their assessments of past events (with a view to future actions), and to do so they particularly use the features upon which dimension 2 is built. On the other hand, speaking time is often sufficient and carefully preplanned for speakers to develop their own narratives. The following speech (chosen at random from the EP_TT corpus) serves as an example of a typical intervention. Note in particular the number of past tense and perfect aspect verbs used:

> Mr President, ladies and gentlemen, this coming 27 January will mark the sixtieth anniversary of the liberation of the concentration camp at Auschwitz. The foundation of the European Coal and Steel Community a few years later **was** a direct consequence of what **had happened** during the Second World War. The fathers and mothers of European cooperation **could** see with their own eyes that ultra-nationalism, Fascism, and the division of our continent by Bolshevism, always **resulted** in oppression, in terror, and in the dignity of the individual being lost. **They could** also see that what **created** peace, dignity and democracy **was** supranational action and integration at a supranational, European level. It is worth adding that this **was** then **achieved** through the Coal and Steel Community gaining control of the weapons-manufacturing industries.
>
> If you trace a continuous line from the ECSC to the European Economic Community, through the next act of integration to the European Community and then to the EU as we know it today, you find a success story as yet unequalled in the world, for it **looked not** only to 1945, and to the end of a war of destruction on this continent; the next stages incorporated states that **had**, in the post-war era, had their own political changes to cope with, namely Greece, Portugal and Spain, and so the overcoming of their fascist dictatorships and the stabilisation of democracy through membership of the European Community **was** an enormous success in the late 1970s and 1980s.
>
> What we saw happening in the 1990s, when the states that **have now acceded took** their present form, was, in principle, a triumph over Communist oppression in one part of Europe. The European Union is a union that **has managed** to take the values described in our Charter

of Fundamental Rights and use them as the basis of democratic integration and to overcome both the Fascism and the Communism of Europe's past.

The events of recent days, in which people **have been** powerless in the face of forces that no amount of technology **has enabled them** to confront, show how absolutely necessary it is for action to be taken at the supranational level, with no national borders standing in the way. In the global village, the European Union is Europe's rational and modern response to the challenges of the twenty-first century. The Constitution we are now debating is the framework provided for it.

Our group will be voting in favour of the Corbett/Méndez de Vigo report – out of profound conviction, and also out of the conviction that the values described in this constitution are civil values. The splendid thing about them is that you can understand them as Christian values if you are a Christian. You can understand them as your own values if you are a Jew or a Moslem or an unbeliever. These values are universal and indivisible, and so they are valid for everyone.

[Martin Schulz on behalf of the PSE group, as translated from German, 11th January, 2005.]

By contrast, the House of Commons meets virtually every day of the year both at the main Chamber and at Westminster Hall. Moreover, a typical form of intervention involves the Chair (Mr/Madam Speaker) allowing MPs to take the floor (for a brief period of time) after they stand up asking to intervene. Short, improvised interventions abound. Everyday meetings seem to justify a discussion of the immediate present or, as *The House of Commons at Work* states, "Many debates relate to day-to-day constituency matters: local hospital services, transport links, planning applications, libraries or an individual's case". Short interventions discourage the narrative presentation of events and tend to encourage quick reactions to critical/laudatory questions about current affairs and especially about the government's performance. An extreme example of this argument is the following intervention, when the speaker (in a very short intervention) discusses not only the immediate present but the very events occurring at the House of Commons:

On a point of order, Mr. Speaker. This is an outrageous abuse. This should be a statement.

[David Maclean (Penrith and The Border) (Con), 10th January 2005]

Why translated speeches are more narrative than original English at the European Parliament begs a closer look that extends beyond the scope of this exploratory study. However, what is clear at this stage is that original and translated English certainly differ along dimension 2 (by over 2 points in their dimension scores), although not quite as much as with HC speeches (which differ from EP production by over 3 points in their dimension scores). This means that according to our data, the communicative setting has a greater impact on variation than the translational process. Another important finding at this exploratory level is that on Biber's dimension 2, it is (again) original speeches made in English that are closest to Biber's spontaneous (with a dimension score of 1.3) and prepared speeches (with a dimension score of 0.7).

Overall, the similarities and differences observed in our ECPC corpora may be (largely) explained by Biber's dimension 2. Notably, the broad span between the narrative nature of EP and HC speeches identified by the MDA methodology is particularly logical considering the rules of procedures for both chambers. MDA also graphically shows narrative distance between EP original and translated speeches, a finding that requires further research within translation studies. In turn, the ECPC corpora contribute to Biber's research, suggesting greater (original and translated) variation within the parliamentary speech genre in English. Our exploratory research also gives rise to questions left unanswered but that fuel inspiration for further research. Among them are the following. (a) Is there further confirmation of the fact that the narrative nature of speeches is influenced by parliamentary settings to a greater extent than by the translational process? (b) Is there further evidence of the finding that past (1960s) speeches from the HC are more faithfully mirrored by present (2005) speeches from the EP? (c) Could a diachronic study of HC speeches better explore why these differ more from Biber's 1960s parliamentary interventions than original EP speeches? (d) Could the difference between the EP_ST and EP_TT corpora suggest a different conception of narration in parliamentary settings or of the role of speakers in parliaments rather than a change in the narrative content of source and target texts?

4.3 Dimension 6

Biber's (1988, p. 107) dimension 6 measures "Online Informational Elaboration". As seen, dimension 6 is related to dimension 1, and we might even conclude that dimension 6 narrows the prism through which linguistic phenomena are seen in dimension 1, weighing down information of especially those texts produced under constrained circumstances. Thus, texts and registers with low scores on this dimension (e.g., personal letter, humour, general fiction, science fiction, mystery and adventure fiction) are viewed as heavily informative and minimally subject to contextual, spontaneous pressures. By contrast, texts and registers with high scores (notably both prepared and spontaneous speeches) are here seen as highly informative but also highly constrained by real-time production circumstances (see De Sutter & Lefer, 2020; Kruger & Van Rooy, 2016). Figure 2.6 captures Biber's dimension 6.

Dimension 6 is based on a very concise list of mainly positive correlation features especially associated with the use of different types of THAT: that clauses as verb complements; that relative clauses; that clauses as adjective complements; and demonstrative pronouns (including that).[3]

In Biber (1988), dimension 6 has strong significance values (F-value = 8.3 and p-value < .0001) and a reasonably high Pearson's correlation factor (r^2 = 28.5%), providing almost a third of the explanation for the arrangement of Figure 2.6. However, Biber (1988, p. 114) find its interpretation to be difficult at times and ends up acknowledging that it requires "further investigation".

For our ECPC corpora, dimension 6 is the second most important determining parameter (after dimension 2). From its vantage point, 2005 (original and translated) EP and HC parliamentary speeches are placed on the gradation depicted in Figure 2.7.

The arrangement of our ECPC corpora along dimension 6 is extremely significant (F-value = 47.2; p-value < 4.031884E-18) and echoes Biber's correlation results (r^2 = 27.5%). These results indicate that almost one-third of the explanations supporting Figure 2.7 are provided by this parameter and that this result is extremely reliable. It might be argued that for TS, dimension 6 has special value due to its connection to the use of (the first type of) THAT, a linguistic feature that has been widely studied in prior research. On the one hand, studies such as Olohan and Baker's (2000) seminal work propose the identification of a much more frequent use of this type of THAT in translations than in original texts. On the other hand, studies such as Delaere and De Sutter (2017) and De Sutter and Lefer (2020) call for more complex (multifactorial) approaches to this object of study.

In our case, the uses and correlations of different types of THAT in translated speeches (from the EP) are clearly and significantly different from those found in original speeches (from the EP and HC). Translations excel in the presence of THAT, while originals rank significantly lower in this respect. Furthermore, in rereading results from dimension 1, which measures, among others, the deletion of THAT in verb complement clauses (e.g., with verbs such as "say" or "tell"), we find that originals from the EP and HC rank higher (and behave more similar to each other) than uses from EP translations. Finally, Biber (1988, p. 243) characterises THAT deletion as "dispreferred in edited writing", relating it to what are seen as unorthodox linguistic constructions.

Parliamentary discourse 49

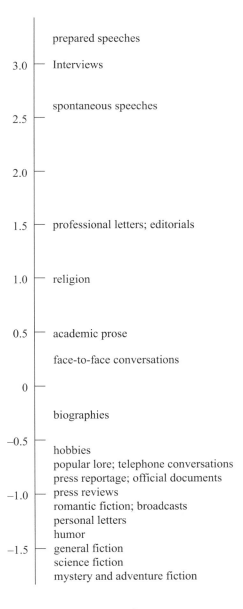

$F = 8.3; p < .0001; r^2 = 28.5\%$

Figure 2.6 Biber's dimension 6

50   *María Calzada-Pérez et al.*

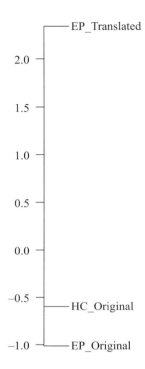

$F = 47.2; p = 4.031884\text{E}{-}18, r^2 = 27.5\%$

Figure 2.7 ECPC (original and translated) subcorpora's dimension 6

Overall, the similarities and differences found in our ECPC corpora may be (largely) explained by Biber's dimension 6. Biber's MDA dimension 6 (and dimension 1) identifies a highly prominent similarity between EP and HC originals in the uses and correlations of different types of THAT regardless of the parliament where speeches are delivered (confirming Olohan & Baker's, 2000 results). Nevertheless, the inclusion of a variety of THAT types in this dimension (and not just in complement to verbs alone) suggests, similar to Delaere and De Sutter (2017) and De Sutter and Lefer (2020), that the issue is more complex than merely the use/deletion of THAT clauses as verb complements and implies that a multifactorial approach, if pursued further, may provide further illustrative explanations for the phenomena. In turn, the ECPC corpora complement Biber's fuzzy and unstable interpretation of dimension 6, which may now be seen under the light of "dispreferred" (Biber, 1988, p. 243) structures in more or less constrained forms of communication. Moreover, as Biber (1988) argues, all dimensions are inextricably connected. The ECPC corpora provide evidence suggesting that dimensions 1 and 6 are closely linked, and results of the former may be elucidated by phenomena detected in the latter, providing new investigative avenues for global analysis, as is the case here. In reviewing dimension 6, the allocation of subcorpora on dimension 1 (which is very closely related to dimension 6) seems more comprehensible than what we initially gathered.

5 Conclusion

With an exploratory and humble spirit, this chapter has compared MDA results for the ECPC Archive (of 2005 original and translated speeches from the EP and HC) to Biber's (1988) seminal research. Due to space constraints, the chapter only comments on three (out of the six) dimensions Biber identifies in 1988 (i.e., dimensions 1, 2 and 6), which prove more illustrative for our exploratory purposes. We set off with the intention to test whether Biber's methodology offers plausible explanations for (original and translated) parliamentary speeches and whether original and translated material could produce valuable insights for Biber's framework. This is performed with a view to contribute to De Sutter and Lefer's (2020) new agenda for empirical translation studies.

Even at this exploratory stage, this chapter suggests that MDA may be seen as a valuable tool for new TS agendas. On each dimension, similarities and differences between the subcorpora are identified. Functional interpretations are then made with what we believe is a high degree of exploratory success. When we gather results from all dimensions, we may build a global account of the texts under study (which are to be pursued further in future research).

In our study, EP_TT texts were found to be particularly informational and narrative and to excel in the orthodox (linguistically preferred) use of THAT (of various types). EP_ST texts were found to be particularly involved and to opt for the unorthodox/linguistically dispreferred use of THAT (of various types). Finally, HC texts appeared as particularly non-narrative and occupied a middle ground (between EP_TT and EP_ST) as per levels of involvement and a preference for orthodoxy in the use of THAT (of various types). As is shown, the translation process could be said to play an important part in the allocation of subcorpora along the dimensions (see dimensions 1 and 6). By contrast, sometimes, it is the context of communicative exchange (the EP or HC in our case) that seems to have a greater impact (as in dimension 2). Plausible reasons for these results are discussed throughout section 4.

In conclusion, from this exploration, synergy between MDA and TS has indisputable advantages, some of which are as follows:

1. Graphically (and statistically) locating subcorpora along each of Biber's dimensions
2. Characterising subcorpora globally with information of all dimensions
3. Identifying objective data that are then to be interpreted with subjectivity based on the overall context of communication

Nevertheless, MDA is certainly not the be-all and end-all of a new agenda for TS for a variety of reasons, among which the following come to mind:

1. (Some) MDA statistical information is not to be regarded as infallible. An r^2 of 2.8% (as in our dimension 1), for example, shows that the results are influenced by a wide range of other possible causes left unstudied by our MDA. However, we equally believe that an r^2 of 2.8% does not mean that the results are to be fully discarded since, after all, they do have a statistically significant impact on the phenomena under study.
2. MDA quantitative data are insufficient to gauge linguistic phenomena on their own; a qualitative (inspiration/imaginative) examination of contexts will be as important in researching in the direction to which statistics point.

Acknowledgements

The present research is funded by the Ministry of Science and Innovation in Spain (PID2019-108866RB-100).

We would like to express our gratitude to Václav Brezina for introducing us to the most technical aspects of multidimensional analysis.

Notes

1 See Biber (1988, pp. 102–103) for a complete summary of factorial structure.
2 See Biber (1988, pp. 102–103) for a complete summary of factorial structure.
3 See Biber (1988, pp. 102–103) for a complete summary of factorial structure.

References

Baker, M. (1993). Corpus linguistics and translation studies: Implications and applications. In M. Baker, G. Francis, & E. Tognini-Bonelli (Eds.), *Text and technology* (pp. 233–250). Amsterdam: John Benjamins Publishing Company.
Berber-Sardinha, T., Kauffman, C., & Mayer-Acunzo, C. (2014). Dimensions of register variation in Brazilian Portuguese. In T. Berber-Sardinha & M. Veirano-Pinto

(Eds.), *Multi-dimensional analysis, 25 years on: A tribute to Douglas Biber* (pp. 35–79). Amsterdam: John Benjamins Publishing Company.

Berber-Sardinha, T., & Veirano-Pinto, M. (Eds.). (2014). *Multi-dimensional analysis, 25 years on: A tribute to Douglas Biber*. Amsterdam: John Benjamins Publishing Company.

Berber-Sardinha, T., & Veirano-Pinto, M. (Eds.). (2019). *Multi-dimensional analysis: Research methods and current issues*. London: Bloomsbury Academic.

Besnier, N. (1988). The linguistic relationships of spoken and written nukulaelae registers. *Language*, *64*(4), 707–736. https://doi.org/10.2307/414565

Biber, D. (1984). *A model of textual relations within the written and spoken modes* (Unpublished doctoral dissertation). Los Angeles: University of Southern California.

Biber, D. (1988). *Variation across speech and writing*. Cambridge: Cambridge University Press.

Biber, D. (1995a). *Dimensions of register variation: A cross-linguistic comparison*. Cambridge: Cambridge University Press.

Biber, D. (1995b). On the role of computational, statistical, and interpretive techniques in multi-dimensional analyses of register variation: A reply to Watson. *Text: Interdisciplinary Journal for the Study of Discourse*, *15*(3), 341–370. https://doi.org/10.1515/text.1.1995.15.3.341

Biber, D. (2014). Multidimensional analysis: A personal history. In T. Berber Sardinha & M. Veirano Pinto (Eds.), *Multi-dimensional analysis, 25 years on: A tribute to Douglas Biber* (pp. xxix–xxxviii). Amsterdam: John Benjamins Publishing Company.

Biber, D. (2019). Multi-dimensional analysis: A historical synopsis. In T. Berber Sardinha & M. Veirano Pinto (Eds.), *Multi-dimensional analysis: Research methods and current issues* (pp. 11–26). London: Bloomsbury Academic.

Biber, D., & Finegan, E. (1992). The linguistic evolution of five written and speech-based English genres from the 17th to the 20th centuries. In M. Rissanen, O. Ihalainen, & T. Nevalainen (Eds.), *History of Englishes: New methods and interpretations in historical linguistics* (pp. 688–704). Berlin: Mouton de Gruyter.

Biber, D., & Hared, M. (1992). Dimensions of register variation in Somali. *Language Variation and Change*, *4*(1), 41–75. https://doi.org/10.1017/S095439450000065X

Brezina, V. (2018). *Statistics in corpus linguistics: A practical guide*. Cambridge: Cambridge University Press. https://doi.org/10.1017/9781316410899

Conrad, S. (2001). Variation among disciplinary texts: A comparison of textbooks and journal articles in biology and history. In S. Conrad & D. Biber (Eds.), *Variation in English: Multi-dimensional studies* (pp. 94–107). Harlow: Pearson.

Delaere, I., & De Sutter, G. (2017). Variability of English loanword use in Belgian Dutch translations: Measuring the effect of source language and register. In G. De Sutter, M. A. Lefer, & I. Delaere (Eds.), *Empirical translation studies: New methodological and theoretical traditions* (pp. 81–112). Berlin: Mouton De Gruyter.

De Sutter, G., & Lefer, M. A. (2020). On the Need for a new research agenda for corpus-based translation studies: A multi-methodological, multifactorial and interdisciplinary approach. *Perspectives*, *28*(1), 1–23. https://doi.org/10.1080/0907676X.2019.1611891

European Parliament. (2019). *The plenary: A user's guide*. www.europarl.europa. eu/sed/doc/ext/manual/Plenary_guide_en.pdf

Friginal, E., & Hardy, J. A. (2019). From factors to dimensions: Interpreting linguistic co-occurrence patterns. In T. Berber Sardinha & M. Veirano Pinto (Eds.), *Multi-dimensional analysis: Research methods and current issues* (pp. 145–164). London: Bloomsbury Academic.

House of Commons. (2018). *House of commons at work*. www.parliament.uk/ documents/commons-information-office/Publications-2015/House-of-Commons-at-work-booklet.pdf

Hu, X., Xiao, R., & Hardie, A. (2016). How do English translations differ from non-translated English writings? A multi-feature statistical model for linguistic variation analysis. *Corpus Linguistics and Linguistic Theory*, *15*(2), 347–382.

Ji, M. (2017). A multidimensional analysis of the translational Chinese genre system. In M. Ji, L. Hereide, D. Li, & M. Oake (Eds.), *Corpus methodologies explained: An empirical approach to translation studies* (pp. 53–102). London: Routledge.

Kenny, D. (1998). Corpora. In M. Baker (Ed.), *Routledge encyclopedia of translation studies* (pp. 50–53). London: Routledge.

Kim, Y., & Biber, D. (1994). A corpus-based analysis of register variation in Korean. In D. Biber & E. Finegan (Eds.), *Sociolinguistic perspectives on register* (pp. 157–181). Oxford: Oxford University Press.

Koskinen, K. (2008). *Translating institutions: An ethnographic study of EU translation*. Manchester: St. Jerome.

Kruger, H. (2019). That again: A multivariate analysis of the factors conditioning syntactic explicitness in translated English. *Across Languages and Cultures*, *20*(1), 1–33.

Kruger, H., & Van Rooy, B. (2016). Constrained language: A multidimensional analysis of translated English and a non-native indigenised variety of English. *English World-Wide*, *37*(1), 26–57.

Laviosa, S. (2011). Corpus-based translation studies: Where does it come from? Where is it going? In Kruger, K. Wallmach, & J. Munday (Eds.), *Corpus-based translation studies: Research and applications* (pp. 13–32). London: Continuum.

Martin, J. R., & White, P. R. R. (2005). *The Language of Evaluation. Appraisal in English*. Basingstoke: Palgrave MacMillan.

Mauranen, A., & Kujamäki, P. (2004). *Translation universals do they exist?* Amsterdam: John Benjamins Publishing Company.

Munday, J. (2012). *Evaluation in translation: Critical points of translator decision-making*. London: Routledge.

Nini, A. (2014). *Multidimensional analysis tagger 1.2: Manual*. http://sites.google.com/site/multidimensionaltagger

Nini, A. (2019). The multi-dimensional analysis tagger. In T. Berber Sardinha & M. Veirano Pinto (Eds.), *Multi-dimensional analysis: Research methods and current issues* (pp. 67–94). London: Bloomsbury Academic.

Olohan, M., & Baker, M. (2000). Reporting that in translated English: Evidence for subconscious processes of explicitation? *Across Languages and Cultures*, *1*(2), 141–158.

Saldanha, G. (2011). Translator style: Methodological considerations. *The Translator*, *17*(1), 25–50. https://doi.org/10.1080/13556509.2011.10799478

Xiao, R. (2009). Multidimensional analysis and the study of world Englishes. *World Englishes*, *28*(4), 421–450. https://doi.org/10.1111/j.1467-971X.2009.01606.x

Xiao, R. (2010). How different is translated Chinese from native Chinese? A corpus-based study of translation universals. *International Journal of Corpus Linguistics*, *15*(1), 5–35.

3 Corpus-based analysis of Russian translations of *Animal Farm* by George Orwell

Mikhail Mikhailov

1 Is it possible to study retranslations with corpus methods?

Habent sua fata libelli. The fate of most literary works is to be published only once and to fall after that into oblivion. Very few are republished and are still read by the next generation. And only in extremely rare cases does the work become a classic, republished many times, read by many generations and sometimes even surviving the language it was written in. A national classic may turn into a world classic, if it is translated into other languages and is popular in different cultures.

The fate of a classical work inside its own culture is dull: its text after a number of editions reaches stability, becomes canonised and mummified and does not change afterwards. This canonical version is faithfully reproduced in academic editions and suffers only minor changes in orthography and punctuation in editions for the general public, the main change being the number of footnotes and endnotes with explanations for the readers.

The fate of a classical work in other cultures is more exciting. After it becomes a world classic, its translations into other languages are also republished, but in many cases old translations are revised and corrected, and after some time entirely new translations come out. Some literary works are translated many times, and new translations continue to appear. For example, Shakespeare's *Othello* was translated into German 38 times from 1766 to 2010 (Alharbi et al., 2015, p. 1). Other works, after being translated several times, reach their canonical form in the target language as well. It is difficult to say whether this is a matter of who and when translated the work or a matter of interest towards the work in the receiving culture.

The reasons for retranslating might be very different. Old translations were often done via a third language and were under the influence of this intermediary language. They were often abridged, and some important passages could have been lost. The translators of the good old days did not have modern dictionaries, encyclopedias and corpora and sometimes made errors

DOI: 10.4324/9781003102694-3

in their translations. Some of the old translations are strongly domesticated (in Venuti's sense, see Venuti 1995), and as a result the original text is hard to recognise. In some cases, the translations were censored or self-censored, which made the translation differ dramatically from the original (see e.g. Desmidt, 2009). Last but not least: the language of the old translations may be hard to understand due to historical changes in the target language.

According to the retranslation hypothesis expressed by Goethe and in 1990 explicitly formulated by Antoine Berman (see e.g. Deane-Cox, 2014, p. 3), retranslations are continuous attempts to reach the ingeniousness of the source text in the target language. They pass various stages: heavily domesticated translations to make the readers acquainted with the work, foreignised translations to make the readers acquainted with the language and structure of the work, and finally – the optimal representation of the source text in this language. However, the hypothesis is difficult to confirm on empirical data. It cannot be taken for granted that each new translation is a step forward: that depends on the translator and other factors. Besides, the quest for producing the best translation is not the only reason for retranslating a work. Many researchers criticise Berman's theory and show that it does not work on their data (e.g. see Deane-Cox, 2014; Kuusi, 2014). At any rate, this hypothesis shows the interrelations between different translations of the same work and the possibility of their influence on each other.

The phenomenon of retranslation of literary works is a topic that has been discussed extensively in translation studies (Venuti 1995; Cadera & Walsh, 2017; Koskinen & Paloposki, 2015; Paloposki & Koskinen, 2010, etc.). A series of conferences with the topic "Retranslation in Context" was initiated in Istanbul in 2013 and successfully continued in 2015 (Istanbul), 2017 (Ghent) and 2019 (Madrid) (Pouke & Gallego, 2019, p. 13). The special issue 27:1 ("Voice in Retranslation") of the journal *Target* was devoted to retranslation. The dominant approach of most publications on the topic is to study retranslating as a cultural rather than as a linguistic phenomenon. For unknown reasons, little use has been made of corpus data in research on this topic, although corpora of retranslated texts would seem to be a natural source of empirical data. Electronic data make it possible to compare different versions, to show how close or distant they are, whether they influenced each other, etc.

Many researchers have studied retranslations by means of manual comparison (e.g. Brownlie, 2006; Desmidt, 2009; Deane-Cox, 2014). Quite a few attempts to use corpus methods for studying multiple translations have been made so far: Jeremy Munday used the WordSmith Tools programme for comparing two English translations of a newspaper article by García Márquez (Munday, 1998); Tom Cheesman, Kevin Flanagan, et al. study in their project "Version, Variation, Visualisation" German translations of Shakespeare's works (Cheesman, Flanagan et al., 2017; Alharbi et al., 2015); Henry Jones analyses English translations of Thucydides using corpus methods (Jones, 2020). There are at least two projects on creating a massively parallel Bible corpus with a thousand or more versions of the Bible in more than 800 languages (Mayer & Cysouw, 2014; McCarthy et al., 2020). The scholars do not however approach the Bible translations from the point of view of translation studies (at least at the present stage) but rather use the resource for typological and contrastive research.

In this chapter, six Russian translations of George Orwell's *Animal Farm* are examined with the help of corpus-based methods. To compare the texts, frequency-list-based distance measure and keywords lists are used. A machine translation of the text performed with Microsoft Translator is used as a baseline for comparison.

2 Methods of studying lexical similarity of texts

To study and compare groups of texts, distance measures can be used. This method can help to get a general picture of the research data, to find which of the texts are closer to each other and which are the most different. The method does not offer any explanations per se, although the researcher can suggest some interpretations. To get deeper into the matter, keyword search can be helpful. While browsing lists of keywords, one can find the actual words that make the text (or a group of texts) in question different from other texts. Keyword search may offer good hints, but it compares texts only pairwise. In my study, I have tried to combine these two methods.

2.1 Distance measures

The most straightforward way to find out how close the texts are is to compare their lexicons. Frequency lists comparison is often used to study corpora or separate texts (see Kilgarriff, 1997, 2001; Piperski, 2017, 2018). The comparison can be based on unlemmatised or lemmatised frequency lists. Using the complete frequency lists does not produce stable results, because a frequency list drawn from a large text would be much longer than that of a short text, and thus long and short texts would be incomparable, and even for texts of the same length low-frequency items would impede the comparison (see also Mikhailov, 2019, pp. 167–168). Therefore, the first X most frequent words (hereafter – MFW) are usually taken. Very short frequency lists would not help to find differences between texts, while very long ones would not work on short texts. In stylometric research MFW 100 (i.e. the first 100 words from frequency lists) is popular (see e.g. Eder et al., 2016).

To measure distances between texts, vectors with normalised frequencies of MFW for each text are composed and a distance matrix of such vectors is

Russian translations of Animal Farm 59

calculated (see Kilgarriff, 1997, 2001, 2008 for details). The next step is to analyse the distance matrix using cluster analysis, multidimensional scaling or some other method. There also exists a *Stylo* package on R that performs stylometric routines on groups of texts (Eder et al., 2016).

In my earlier research (Mikhailov, 2019) I have demonstrated that translations of the same works tend to be lexically very close, and a frequency-list-based distance measure makes it possible to distinguish retranslations of the same texts from other translated and non-translated texts (e.g. same author, same topic etc.). This finding is not surprising: the texts based on the same source text are of approximately the same length and have many overlaps in vocabulary. When studying retranslations, differences between texts are more important than similarities. Are there clusters of texts that are closer to each other? Why do some texts become outliers? Usually these are old translations, but can there be exceptions? Frequency-list-based distance measures yield only a very general picture without telling the researcher what is particularly different in the texts compared.

2.2 Keyword analysis

A more detailed analysis of the differences in vocabulary between retranslations can be performed with the help of keyword lists. Keywords are words from the research data that have frequencies significantly different from their frequencies in the reference corpus (Mikhailov & Cooper, 2016, pp. 133–144). Keyword analysis is very popular: it is used in many fields of linguistics, digital humanities and translation studies (see e.g. Čermakova & Farova, 2010; Fidler & Cvrček, 2015; Johnson & Esslin, 2006; Kemppanen, 2004, 2008; Milizia, 2010; Seale et al., 2006; Wilkinson, 2014).

The popular software package WordSmith Tools has a Keywords utility that can be used for getting lists of keywords for single texts or collections of texts (Scott & Tribble, 2006, https://lexically.net/downloads/version8/HTML/keywords.html). The SketchEngine online tool also has a Keywords utility that can be used for querying the ready-made corpora or users' own text collections (www.sketchengine.eu/my_keywords/keyword/). Also, keywords lists can be extracted from two frequency word lists with the help of any statistical package (R, SPSS etc) or even with spreadsheet software like Microsoft Excel or Libre Office Calc.

In fact, there exist many alternative ways to compute the "keyness": chi-square and log-likelihood, among others. The simplest method available is surprisingly effective; this is Adam Kilgarriff's simple measure (Kilgarriff, 2009), which is calculated with the formula:

$K = (Fe + N)/(Fc + N)$,

where *Fe* and *Fc* are the relative frequencies of the item in the experimental and control data (e.g. expressed in items per million, ipm), and *N* is a smoothing parameter, a constant. Smaller *N* (e.g. 1, 10) emphasises high-frequency words, larger *N* (e.g. 100, 1,000) puts more weight on medium- and low-frequency words. This measure is widely used in the Sketch Engine (sketchengine.eu) and other corpus tools.

Keywords are easily applicable to the comparison of translations (see e.g. Čermakova & Farova, 2010). A list of keywords for a pair of translations of the same source text reveals what is particularly different in these texts. The list shows what words the given translator loves to use, what words he/she uses more often than the other translator, and what words he/she is trying to get rid of. The length and the structure of the list can expose the extent of dependence of the new translation on the old one: whether the new translation is just an edited and corrected old translation, or the new translation is heavily based on the old translation, or whether the new translation is really new.

3 Comparing retranslations using corpus methods. *Animal Farm* in Russian

When comparing a group of objects, it is good to have a starting point, an ideal object to compare with. It is very difficult to choose such a starting point for a group of translations of the same text. Each case is unique: some of older translations influence new translations, some are completely forgotten, some new translations are based on previous translations, some are performed without consulting any previous works. The quality might be improving in new translations, or it may remain the same or even degrade. Therefore, choosing the first or the last translation as a hub for comparison would not work in many cases.

The best starting point would have been the original text, but it is written in another language, and this makes comparison impossible. A literal translation of the original into the target language would have been a good solution, but this is too difficult technically, especially with long texts. A machine translation of the text would ostensibly be the closest to a literal translation and can be used therefore as a kind of 'projection' of the source text onto another language. Such a projection would not be an ideal one: a machine-translated text contains lexical and grammatical errors, as well as wrong translation equivalents. Still, it has certain strengths: it is standardised, neutral and easy to obtain. For these reasons I decided to add a machine-translated version to the human translations and use it as a baseline for comparison.

3.1 The research data

As it has been already mentioned, this chapter is devoted to the analysis of the Russian translations of George Orwell's *Animal Farm* (1945). The original text was aligned at the sentence level with a machine translation and six human translations. The software used for aligning was LF Aligner (https://sourceforge.net/projects/aligner/). The aligned texts were parsed with universal dependencies grammar parsers (https://universaldependencies.org/). The corpus software I used for querying the data was TextHammer, a web-based corpus manager that I developed myself (puolukka.rd.tuni.fi/texthammer).

The machine translation was performed with Microsoft Translator via WordFast translation memory programme. The resulting translation in the form of aligned bitexts was exported to a TMX file that was easy to parse and upload to the corpus database.

The human translations that are studied in this mini-research are the translations by Struve and Kriger (1949), Pribylovskij (1986), Task (1988), Polotsk (1989), Kibirskij (1989) and Bespalova (1989) (see Appendix for details). According to the FantLab website (FantLab, n.d.), there exist at least two more Russian translations of Orwell's story, but these were not available.

It is easy to notice that five of these six translations were made almost at the same time, and it is quite possible that the translators did not even know that other new translations of the same book were being prepared. The translators of the 1980s might have been familiar with the first Russian translation by Struve and Kriger, which was published in West Germany by Posev publishing house (some copies were smuggled to the Soviet Union; the book was prohibited in the USSR until Perestroika), and might have been consulting it while translating. To check this, a search for matching segments in the translations was performed. For this purpose, a PHP-script was developed by the author of this chapter. The search shows that none of the later translations contain extensive borrowings from the first translation. The largest amount of closely matching sentences longer than two words with Dice index greater than 70% was found in the translations by Pribylovskij (101 sentences) and Kibirskij (108 sentences). The total number of sentences in the translations vary from 1,733 to 1,804; thus, the percentage of such possible borrowings is very low, a little more than 5%. The translation by Polotsk contains much fewer matches – 60 – and even less were found in the translations by Task (41) and Bespalova (27).

Among the matches found are sentences that could have been produced by the translators independently, e.g. *Vse životnye ravny* 'All animals are equal'. However, some longer extracts do not look to be mere coincidences.

1   No animal must ever live in a house, or sleep in a bed, or wear clothes, or drink alcohol, or smoke tobacco, or touch money, or engage in trade. (Orwell)
1a Не живите в домах, не спите на кроватях, не носите одежды, не пейте спиртного, не курите, не занимайтесь торговлей, не берите в руки денег. (Bespalova)
1b Ни одно животное не должно жить в доме, спать в кровати, носить одежду, пить алкогольные напитки, курить табак, прикасаться к деньгам, заниматься торговлей. (Kibirskij)
1c Ни одно из животных не должно жить в доме, спать в постели, носить одежду, пить алкоголь, курить табак, притрагиваться к деньгам или заниматься торговлей. (Polotsk)
1d Ни одно животное не должно жить в доме, спать в постели, носить одежду, не должно употреблять алкоголь и курить табак, заниматься торговлей и вести денежные расчеты. (Task)
1e Ни одно животное не должно жить в доме, спать в кровати, носить одежду, пить спиртное, курить, прикасаться к деньгам, торговать. (Pribylovskij)
1f Ни одно животное не должно жить в доме или спать в постели, носить одежду, пить спиртное, курить табак, прикасаться к деньгам или торговать. (Struve & Kriger)

In example (1) the translations 1b, 1c and 1e almost coincide with 1f. Of course, the sentence of the source text has simple and transparent structure and vocabulary and therefore can stimulate similar translations, especially if translators use the same dictionaries and have similar backgrounds.

However, the possibility of using a standard solution by the translators in example (2) does not look very convincing.

2   As he had said, his voice was hoarse, but he sang well enough, and it was a stirring tune, something between 'Clementine' and 'La Cucaracha'. (Orwell)
2a Голос у него, и верно, был сиплый, но пел он неплохо. И мотив, помесь "Клементины" и "Кукарачи", брал за сердце. (Bespalova)
2b Голос его и вправду звучал сипло, но пел он довольно хорошо. Мотив был бодрый и волнующий (нечто среднее между мелодиями "Клементайна" и "Ла Кукарачча"). (Kibirskij)
2c Как он и говорил, голос у него был хриплый, но волнующая мелодия, нечто среднее между "Клементиной" и "Кукарачей" звучала достаточно чисто. (Polotsk)

2d Хотя голос у него и вправду был уже не тот, однако пел он довольно прилично, и мелодия сразу западала в сердце, напоминая одновременно "Клементину" и "Кукарачу". (Task)
2e Как он и предупреждал, голос у него был хриплый, но пел он совсем неплохо, и мотив у песни был бодрый, что-то среднее между "Клементиной" и "Кукарачей". (Pribylovskij)
2f Как он сам сказал, голос у него был хриплый, но пел он совсем не плохо, а мотив был бодрящий – нечто среднее между "Клементиной" и "Кукарачей". (Struve & Kriger)

The source sentence in the example (2) is longer and more complicated both lexically and syntactically, but still 2a, 2c and 2e match 2f, while 2a and 2d are different.

We can therefore suppose that Pribylovskij, Kibirskij and Polotsk did use to some extent the translation by Struve and Kriger, while Task and Bespalova evidently worked only with the source text.

3.2 The visual impressions

Unlike a normal corpus-based study, our research data is just seven versions of one relatively short text, and this makes it possible to cast a glance at the translations and to form an opinion on their quality.

3.2.1 The machine translation

The machine translation is (quite expectedly) unacceptable for publishing, although one must admit that the level achieved by the programme in some passages is surprisingly good. In a short extract demonstrated in Table 3.1, only segment (2) is acceptable, albeit somewhat heavy stylistically. Other segments need minor or major corrections. Segment (1) contains a grammatically incorrect construction *byla prinjata . . . rešenie* (the verbal clause is in feminine while the object is a neuter noun, the correct form: *bylo prinjato . . . rešenie*). Segment (3) has a redundant *sozvali ih vmeste*, the verb *sozvat'* 'to call together' has a seme 'to gather' included into its meaning and thus the adverb *vmeste* 'together' only complicates and disbalances the sentence. Segment (4) contains constructions that are grammatically unacceptable: *eto polovina šestogo* (should be *sejčas polovina šestogo*) and *u nas est' dlinnyj den' pered nami* (correct version: *pered nami dlinnyj den'*). The punctuation of the sentence is not quite correct either. In Russian, direct speech is signalled with m-dashes, and the punctuation in (4) should have been like this: *"Direct speech", – indirect speech, – "direct*

Table 3.1 A fragment of a bitext with machine translation

	Source text (Orwell)	Machine translation (Microsoft Translator)
1	A unanimous resolution was passed on the spot that the farmhouse should be preserved as a museum.	На месте была принята единогласное решение о том, что фермерский дом должен быть сохранен как музей.
2	All were agreed that no animal must ever live there.	Все были согласны с тем, что ни одно животное никогда не должно жить там.
3	The animals had their breakfast, and then Snowball and Napoleon called them together again.	Звери позавтракали, а потом Снежок и Наполеон снова созвали их вместе.
4	"Comrades," said Snowball, "it is half-past six and we have a long day before us.	"Товарищи", сказал Снежок, "это половина шестого, и у нас есть длинный день перед нами.
5	Today we begin the hay harvest.	Сегодня мы начинаем урожай сена.
6	But there is another matter that must be attended to first."	Но есть еще один вопрос, который должен быть принят в первую очередь".

speech continued". In the segments (5) and (6), wrong lexemes are chosen: *urožaj* 'crops' (should be *uborka* 'gathering' or *uborka urožaja* 'gathering of crops') and *prinjat* 'decided' (should be *rešen* 'settled').

As a whole, the machine translation is in most cases readable and understandable (although some passages sound comical), but it does not make a cohesive text: each segment is handled by the programme separately, without taking into account the information from previous segments. As a result, proper names are not translated consistently, e.g. names of the characters like *Boxer* or *Clover* regularly turn into common nouns. Gender of the characters floats from masculine to feminine and back. The style does not meet the standards of a literary text, it is not consistent and grades from official to colloquial. Also, when translating passages with complex syntax, the programme makes grammar errors and confuses equivalents.

Still, in spite of its insufficient quality and numerous errors, the machine translation closely follows the structure of the source text and makes no omissions, which makes it suitable for the role of a starting point for comparison of the human translations.

3.2.2 The human translations

It was fairly difficult to rate the Russian translations by reading impressions. The earliest translation by Struve and Kriger looks rather old-fashioned;

some words used in the translation have changed their meaning in the modern language (e.g. *šosse* in the meaning 'any road' which means in modern Russian 'a motorway'), and there are small omissions because the translators evidently used an earlier edition of the Orwell's work. The later translations are roughly on the same level and all have their own strengths and weaknesses. The translations by Sergei Task and S. Kibirskij are more domesticated, the translation by Ilan Polotsk is more foreignised; in any case, none of the translations can be called clearly domesticated or clearly foreignised: all contain both trends. The translators are switching constantly between copying English syntax and rewriting some passages completely, transliterating some names and translating others, replacing English realia by Russian realia and preserving English realia, etc.

3   Remove Man from the scene, and the root cause of hunger and overwork is abolished for ever. (Orwell)
3a Если мы уберем человека, мы навеки покончим с голодом и непосильным трудом, ибо человек – их причина. (Bespalova)
3b Удалите Человека – и основная причина голода и рабского положения животных будет устранена навеки. (Kibirskij)
3c Уберите со сцены человека, и навсегда исчезнет причина голода и непосильного труда. (Polotsk)
3d Уберите с подмостков Истории человека, и вы навсегда покончите с голодом и рабским трудом. (Task)
3e Уберите Человека – и коренная причина голода и изнурительных трудов будет устранена навеки. (Pribylovskij)
3f Уберите Человека, и коренная причина голода и переутомления будет устранена навеки. (Struve & Kriger)

In example (3) one can see how the same phrase is treated by different translators. As in the previous examples, a certain similarity can be traced between the translation by Struve and Kriger (3f), Pribylovskij (3e), and Kibirskij (3b). The translations by Kibirskij (3b), Polotsk (3c), Pribylovskij (3e) and Struve and Kriger (3f) follow the structure and even try to preserve some features of orthography (capitalised *Man*) and punctuation (comma before *and*) of the original. In contrast, Bespalova (3a) makes changes in syntax and makes the statement more explicit. Kibirskij (3b) changes *overwork* of the source text to *rabskoe položenie* 'slavery conditions'. Task (3e) preserves syntactic structure but makes radical semantical changes (e.g. *scene* → *podmostki Istorii* 'the stage of History').

Interestingly, in general the translations look after all surprisingly different. There are different ways of translating the title of the book (see Table 3.2), the names of the personages (e.g. *Snowball*: *Snežok* 'snowball'

Table 3.2 *Animal Farm* and its translations

Author (translator)	Title	Year	Number of editions	Number of sords	Number of characters	Length of lemmatised word list	STTR
Orwell, George	Animal Farm	1945		30,437	138,269	3,556	48.4
Microsoft Translator	Ferma životnyh	–		25,027	136,521	3,859	64.39
Struve, Gleb & Kriger, Marina	Skotskij hutor	1949	2	22,746	125,839	4,280	67.76
Pribylovskij V.	Ferma životnyh	1986	3	23,729	133,657	4,830	69.65
Task, Sergey	Skotskij ugolok	1988	10	21,399	122,690	5,038	73.33
Bespalova, Larisa	Skotnyj dvor	1989	29	23,004	125,250	4,655	67.49
Kibirskij, S.	Ferma životnyh	1989	2	23,085	131,400	4,472	70.3
Polotsk, Ilan	Skotskij hutor	1989	1	23,879	134,518	4,319	67.42

(Struve & Kriger, Pribylovskij, Kibirskij), *Ciceron* 'Cicero' (Task), *Obval* 'avalanche' (Bespalova), *Snouboll* (Polotsk)), other proper names (e.g. the *animalism* doctrine: *skotizm* 'cattle + ism' (Struve & Kriger, Bespalova), *zverizm* 'beast + ism' (Pribylovskij), *animalizm* (Kibirskij, Polotsk, Task)). Despite this, publishers seem to prefer two translations: by Larisa Bespalova (29 editions) and by Sergey Task (10 editions) (see Table 3.2). In spite of this fact, one cannot claim that the Bespalova's translation has met all the standards of an ideal translation because it is the most popular.

Visual comparison of different translations of the same text yields many interesting observations. Yet it is not possible to obtain a general picture of the continuum made up of attempts to acquire the best translation. Only quantitative data may give a clue.

3.3 Descriptive statistics

Let us have a look, if descriptive statistics can shed more light on the matter. In Table 3.2 the information on the original text of the story and its translations can be found. I have provided four measures: number of words, number of characters, length of lemmatised word list and standardised type-token ratio per 1,000 words (STTR, see explanation later in the chapter).

Eugen Nida and Charles Taber claim that a translation will be always longer than an original text, because the translator has to make explicit many things that are evident to the readers of the source text (Nida & Taber, 1974, p. 163). This heuristic is very difficult to confirm or refute, because different languages have their own ways of 'packing' the information: short words vs. long words, synthetic vs. analytical grammar forms, use of composite words, use of particles, use of articles, etc. In any case, the data from this case study does not confirm this heuristic. The number of words in the Russian translations is much less than in the original text, the main reason being that Russian is an articleless language. The difference in number of characters is smaller; even so the Russian translations are 'shorter' than the English original.

It follows from the Nida and Taber heuristic that a machine translation (that is generated mechanically and is incapable to make implicit information explicit) should be shorter than a human translation (that is created having in mind the background of the audience). Strangely, in our data the machine translation is much longer than any human translation (see Table 3.2). Probably the reason is that human translators are able to find alternative ways of translating complicated constructions while the machine translator has no option but to go the straight way and is therefore forced to use long and clumsy solutions. The lengths of the human translations vary between 122,690 characters (Task) and 134,519 characters (Polotsk), which confirms that the length of a translation has something to do with preserving the structure of the source text in the translation and with smoothing of angles. As has been mentioned earlier, the first is the most domesticated and the last the most foreignised translation.

The STTR index (the mean of the ratio of number of unique words (types) to number of different words (tokens) calculated for fix-length extracts, e.g. 1,000 words; see Mikhailov & Cooper, 2016, pp. 116–121 for a detailed explanation) shows diversity of vocabulary and thus reflects repetitiveness, readability and lexical richness. Texts with low STTR are more simple, more straightforward, easier to read, but dull and repetitive, while texts with high STTR are more compact, less repetitive, more attractive, but more difficult to read. STTR values for different languages are different; therefore the lower value of STTR of the original English text in Table 3.2 does not mean that the Russian translations are 'more beautiful'. After comparing STTR values of the translations we can make an interesting observation: the machine translation has much lower STTR than the human translations. This is what we could have expected. The STTR values of the human translations vary from 67.49 (Bespalova) to 73.33 (Task). Strangely, these two translations with the extreme values of STTR are also the most often published (see section 3.2). Anyway, the difference in STTR values of human translations is not significant.

To sum up the findings, the numeric data reveals much more variation than might be expected from the translations of the same work. Still, no conclusions can be drawn yet from these number without more sophisticated data processing.

3.4 Studying retranslations with distance measure

One of the ways to get deeper into the matter would be measuring distances between the translations, as was described in section 2.1. To obtain the data for the distance measuring, I generated lemmatised frequency lists of all seven texts (machine translation and six human translations), than loaded the lists in R.[1] As was already mentioned in section 2.1, comparing complete lists is not very effective even for related texts; therefore the lists were truncated to the 100 most frequent words. The truncated lists were merged into a single table, the table was rotated and the final dataset was a data frame with data on texts in rows and words in columns (see a fragment in Table 3.3). The frequencies were normalised to items per thousand.[2] Full outer join was used for merging of the tables, that is, items that did not occur in all frequency lists were also copied to the new table. The size of the resulting data frame was 7 × 155.

On the next stage, I generated a distance matrix and performed multidimensional scaling (MDS) on it. The software used were R Studio and its

Table 3.3 A fragment from the joint frequency table

	a: CCONJ	*боец*: NOUN	*бой*: NOUN	*больше*: ADV	*большой*: ADJ	*бы*: PART	*быть*: AUX	*быть*: VERB
Bespalova	9.61	4.48	1.39	0	0	3.43	8.87	2.39
Kibirskij	5.93	0	0	1.52	1.6	1.91	18.45	2.6
MT	2.64	0	0	0	2.24	2.56	37.2	3.32
Polotsk	4.4	0	0	0	0	1.93	19.81	2.68
Pribylovskij	7.33	0	0	0	1.39	2.36	15	3.41
Struve & Kriger	5.14	0	0	0	0	2.42	23.17	3.3
Task	6.87	0	0	0	0	2.66	12.9	2.29

packages *cluster* and *smacof*. The MDS analysis worked well; the stress value was 1.3, which generally means that the fit of the two-dimensional model is good. The resulting visualisation can be seen in Figure 3.1. The texts are placed into a two-dimensional space; the geometrical distances between the dots reflect the differences between the frequencies of their MFWs. The lowest value on the x-axis get the machine translation, the highest – the translations by Bespalova and Task, which, as was already mentioned, are also the most popular (see section 3.2).

Probably the x-axis is related to preserving the structure of the original text: the extreme case is the machine translation with minimal changes, while the translations by Bespalova and Task contain changes in structure, possible omissions and explicitations for making the text more transparent and more readable.

As it was already mentioned in section 3.2, the visual inspection of the texts left the impression that Bespalova tried to adapt the structure of the translation to the norms of Russian style, while Task's translation is very free and changes on semantic level happen fairly often. It is possible

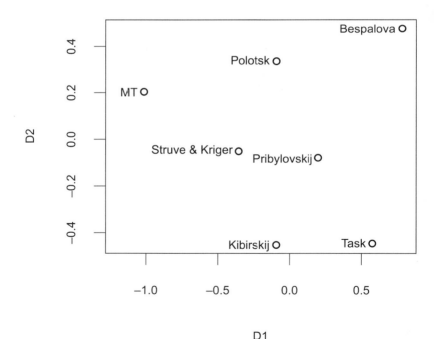

Figure 3.1 Distance measure visualisation (MDS)

therefore that the y-axis shows the gradation from grammatical changes to lexical changes.

The human translation closest to MT both on the x and y axes is the translation by Struve and Kriger. The position on the x-axis shows that this is the most literal translation in our group, and the position on the y-axis means that the structure of the source text is mostly preserved and some minor lexical changes may be found.

3.4 Keywords analysis of retranslations

Keywords help to figure out which items are specific for the research data. Keywords are not an absolute concept; they are always relative to the reference data. When performing searches for keywords, it is vitally important to choose a relevant reference data set; the resulting list largely depends on this choice. The selection of the reference corpus should be made keeping in mind the objectives of the study. When comparing the research data against a large corpus of general language, the keyword list would tell about the topic and the text type, when the reference corpus consists of texts of the same text type, the keywords would show the specifics of the subgenre or of the style of the author.

In this study, the task is to find out how the translations of the same work differ one from another. Using a large corpus of language for general purposes as reference data would not provide an answer to the question: the lists obtained from retranslations would be close to each other, and the differences would be blurred. Using one of the translations should be more effective, but the question is which translation to take. Fortunately, we have a machine translation, which is the most literal and has neither omissions nor additions, so we can use the machine translation as the reference data.

Keyword search was run on lemmatised word lists using Kilgarriff's simple measure with $N = 100$ (see section 2.2.) and the items with $K \geq 2$ were taken. Proper names were removed from the results. A fragment of one of the keyword lists can be seen in Table 3.3.

3.4.1 The keyword lists: general information

One would expect that the lists obtained this way would be very close. This did not happen, however. Only four (!) items are present in all six keyword lists: *vot* 'this is, interj.', *zerno* 'grain, n', *korovnik* 'cowshed, n', *tvoj* 'your, pron. 2 pers. Sg'.

Keyword lists often help to find interesting lexical items in the data and observe its specific features. Indeed, it is easy to notice that the keyword list of the translation by Struve and Kriger contains many archaic words like *ibo* 'because', *glasit'* 'to announce', *javit'sja* 'to appear'. As for other translations, their keyword lists do not seem to contain anything special. Let us try therefore to study those lists as a whole.

The shortest list was the list of keywords for the translation by Struve and Kriger (57 items) and the longest were the lists for the translations by Task (118), Polotsk (84) and Bespalova (83) (see Table 3.4). Thus, the keyword search goes in line with the results of the MDS analysis of the frequency lists carried out in section 3.3.

We can anticipate that the more differences there are between experimental and reference data, the larger keyness values (i.e. values of K) they would have. The keyness values for the top ten keywords in our lists vary from 5.72 to 3.24 (Struve & Kriger), 6.56 to 3.42 (Kibirskij), 9.44 to 3.42 (Polotsk), 7.87 to 2.83 (Pribylovskij), 12.65 to 4.16 (Bespalova) and 7.71 to 4.21 (Task). Hence, the keywords from the translation by Struve and Kriger have the lowest keyness values, while the values of those from the translations by Bespalova and Task are the highest.

3.4.2 Cohesion words

The weak point of MT is text cohesion. A machine translator handles pronouns, conjunctions and particles of the source text in the same way as any other items (nouns, verbs, adjectives), while human translators obviously choose first a suitable syntactic construction and use the grammatical markers it needs: for a compound sentence a conjunction would be needed, a nominalised clause would do with a preposition. That is why all six keyword lists contain pronouns, conjunctions, particles and prepositions. The amount of such items signals the extent of adaptation of syntax to the norms of the

Table 3.4 A fragment of the keyword list from the translation by Struve & Kriger

Token	Experimental data, ipm	Reference data, ipm	K
сражение 'battle'	923.00	79.00	5.72
работник 'worker'	483.00	39.00	4.19
всякий 'any'	967.00	159.00	4.12
коровник 'cowshed'	615.00	79.00	3.99
прежний 'of the previous times'	439.00	39.00	3.88
дерево 'tree'	527.00	79.00	3.50
заказ 'order'	659.00	119.00	3.47
уметь 'be able'	483.00	79.00	3.26
употреблять 'to use'	351.00	39.00	3.24

target language. The study of keyword lists shows that the list from the translation of Struve and Kriger contains the fewest cohesion words. The lists of keywords from the translations by Polotsk, Kibirskij and Pribylovskij also do not contain many words of these kinds, while among keyword lists from the translations by Bespalova and especially by Task many pronouns, particles and even prepositions can be found (see Table 3.5).

Emphasizing particle *vot* 'here is' can be found in all keywords lists. English has much fewer particles than Russian and uses other markers to highlight elements of the text. Therefore *vot* occurs only three times in the machine translation and is quite frequent in the human translations, especially in the translations by Bespalova (61 occurrences) and Task (34 occurrences).

4   Man is the only real enemy we have. (Orwell)
4a Человек – <u>вот</u> кто наш истинный враг. (Bespalova)
4b Человек – наш единственный подлинный враг. (Kibirskij)
4c <u>Вот</u> кто наш единственный подлинный враг – человек. (Polotsk)
4d <u>Вот</u> он, корень зла – человек. Другого врага у нас нет. (Task)
4e Человек – <u>вот</u> наш единственный подлинный враг. (Pribylovskij)
4f Человек – <u>вот</u> наш единственный настоящий враг. (Struve & Kriger)
4e Человек – единственный настоящий враг, который у нас есть. (MT)

In example (4) only Kibirskij does not use *vot* in the translation. Obviously, without it the statement loses energy. The machine translation (4e) is grammatically and lexically correct and is the closest variant of translation; still, not one of human translators chosen this way of translating this sentence.

The particle *vot* is obviously a favourite of Bespalova; the relative frequency of the word in her translation is 2,651.71 ipm, which is much

Table 3.5 Part of speech statistics in the keyword lists

Tokens	Bespalova	Kibirskij	Polotsk	Pribylovskij	Struve & Kriger	Task
a	4	10	7	9	4	12
adv	10	9	9	6	6	11
conj	1	1	0	1	1	1
n	26	23	28	23	16	47
particles	9	7	4	6	4	9
prep	3	2	2	2	0	3
pron	7	3	6	6	4	9
v	23	22	28	14	22	26
Total	**83**	**77**	**84**	**67**	**57**	**118**

higher than in the Russian National Corpus (1785.1 ipm; see Ljaševskaja & Šarov, 2009).

5   The words ran: (Orwell)
5a Вот эта песня: (Bespalova)
5b Слова же были такие: (Kibirskij)
5c Слова были таковы: (Polotsk)
5d Впрочем, ближе к тексту: (Task)
5e Слова были таковы: (Pribylovskij)
5f Слова же были следующие: (Struve & Kriger)
5e Слова побежал: (MT)

In example (5) only Bespalova inserts *vot* in translation. The original text looks very simple, although the direct translation suggested by MT (5e) is impossible, and not only because of disagreement of the noun and the verb: the verb *pobežat'* 'to start running' is never used in the meaning 'to express by means of language'. Still, only two translators, Polotsk (5c) and Pribylovskij (5e) do not use any particles in their translations. Bespalova uses *vot*, Kibirskij (5b) and Struve and Kriger (5f) use another particle, *že*, Task (5d) starts the sentence with a modal word *vpročem* 'however'.

These examples show that the cohesion words are in most cases added by translator and not transferred from the original text. Use of these markers belongs to individual style of translator.

3.4.3 Nouns and verbs

The faithfulness of the translations to the original correlates with the numbers of nouns in the lists of keywords: the smallest number is in the translation by Struve and Kriger, the largest is in the translation by Task (see Table 3.5). An interesting feature of the keyword lists of the translations by Task and by Pribylovskij is that the number of nouns is almost two times bigger than that of verbs, while for the remaining four translations the number of nouns and verbs in the keyword lists is almost equal. Where do all these nouns come from?

One of the most frequent nouns of the keyword list from the translation by Task is *massa* 'mass': it occurs only twice in the MT and the translation by Polotsk, only once in the translation by Kibirskij and is never used in other translations. Task uses the word *massa* in two meanings: 'a large group of people' and 'physical mass'. The first usage (in plural) is very typical for Marxist literature (at least in Russian), and Task uses the word to link the *Animal Farm* to a socialist state. However, Orwell does not use the word *mass*; therefore, Task's use of the word *massa* signals changes in the content of the source text.

Russian translations of Animal Farm 75

6   These two had great difficulty in thinking anything out for themselves, but having once accepted the pigs as their teachers, they absorbed everything that they were told, and <u>passed it on to the other animals</u> by simple arguments. (Orwell)

6a Они ничего не могли придумать самостоятельно, но, раз и навсегда признав свиней своими учителями, буквально впитывали каждое их слово и доходчиво передавали <u>другим животным</u>. (Bespalova)

6b Им обоим было трудно самостоятельно всё продумать, но, однажды признав свиней своими учителями, они впитывали всё, что им говорилось, и затем передавали это простыми словами <u>другим животным</u>. (Kibirskij)

6c Сам процесс мышления доставлял им немалые трудности, но раз и навсегда признав свиней своими пастырями, Кловер и Боксер впитывали в себя все, что было ими сказано и затем терпеливо втолковывали это <u>остальным животным</u>. (Polotsk)

6d Эти двое были не способны дойти до чего-либо своим умом, но после того как им все разжевали, они стали самыми надежными проводниками свинских идей; они <u>внедряли их в сознание масс</u> с помощью простейших формулировок. (Task)

6e Они с огромным трудом могли бы что-нибудь придумать сами, но признав однажды свиней своими учителями, они принимали все, что те говорили, на веру и в доходчивых выражениях объясняли это <u>другим животным</u>. (Pribylovskij)

6f Этим двум не легко было мыслить самим, но, раз уже признав свиней своими учителями, они усваивали все, что им говорили, и с помощью простых доводов передавали усвоенное <u>другим животным</u>. (Struve & Kriger)

In example (6) Task replaces *other animals* by *massy* 'masses', while other translations just keep to the original using direct equivalents: *drugie/ostal'nye životnye* 'other/remaining animals'.

7   Napoleon sent for pots of black and white paint and <u>led the way</u> down to the five-barred gate that gave on to the main road. (Orwell)

7a Наполеон распорядился принести по банке черной и белой краски и <u>повел их</u> к тесовым воротам, выходящим на большак. (Bespalova)

7b Наполеон послал за черной и белой краской и <u>подвел всех</u> к тяжелым воротам, отгораживавшим ферму от дороги. (Kibirskij)

7c Наполеон послал за банками с черной и белой красками и <u>направился</u> к воротам, за которыми начиналась основная дорога. (Polotsk)

7d Наполеон послал Делового за масляной краской, черной и белой, а сам повел массы к главным воротам. (Task)
7e Наполеон послал за ведрами с черной и белой краской и повел всех вниз, к выходившим на главную дорогу воротам, которые были окованы пятью железными скрепами. (Pribylovskij)
7f Наполеон послал за банками черной и белой краски и провел животных к калитке, которая выходила на шоссе. (Struve & Kriger)

In example (7) the word *massy* appears in Task's translation out of nowhere: in the original text the object is implicit, *led the way*. Struve and Kriger (7f) explicitate it as *provel životnyh* 'led the animals'; Polotsk (7c) removed the object completely, changing the verb to *napravilsja* 'went'; other translators explicitate the object by adding a pronoun: *povel vseh* 'led all'. Task changes the neutral source text to pathetic *povel massy* 'led the masses'.

8 Without halting for an instant, Snowball flung his fifteen stone against Jones's legs. (Orwell)
8a Но Обвал не дрогнул и всей своей шестипудовой тушей двинул Джонса по ногам. (Bespalova)
8b Ни на мгновение не замедляя бега, Снежок врезался всеми своими девяноста пятью килограммами в колени врага. (Kibirskij)
8c Ни на мгновенье не останавливаясь, Сноуболл всем своим внушительным весом сбил Джонса с ног. (Polotsk)
8d Не сбавляя хода, Цицерон всей своей массой врезал Джонсу по ногам. (Task)
8e Ни на секунду не останавливаясь, Снежок налетел на фермера и все шесть пудов своего веса бросил ему под ноги. (Pribylovskij)
8f Не останавливаясь ни на секунду, Снежок бросил свою пятипудовую тушу под коленки Джонсу. (Struve & Kriger)

In example (8) Task uses the word *massa* in the different meaning, and it is used as equivalent for a culture-specific word *stone* (an English unit of weight). None of the translators try to preserve this word in the translation. Bespalova (8a), Pribylovskij (8e) and Struve and Kriger convert stones into *puds* (pud is a traditional Russian weight measure, 16 kg), Kibirskij (8b) converts stones into kilograms, and others just mention that Snowball was heavy: *svoim vnušitel'nym vesom* 'with his impressive weight' (Polotsk, 8c), *vsej svoej massoj* 'with all his mass' (Task, 8d).

No great variety can be observed in the numbers of verbs in the lists of keywords: all lists have between 20 and 30 verbs, with the exception of Pribylovskij's translation, which has only 14. The verbs from the keyword list of Pribylovskij are more abstract than the verbs from other five lists. No verbs of action can be found; there are verbs of social activities (*rukovodit'* 'to manage', *gotovit'* 'to prepare', *sledit'* 'to spy'), verbs of speech (*uverjat'* 'to assure', *priznavat'sja* 'to confess') and verbs of state (*otnosit'sja* 'to belong', *predstojat'* 'to expect'). In contrast, the verbs of the keyword lists from other translations are not only more numerous but also more diverse; for example, in Bespalova's keyword list there are verbs of action (*snesti* 'to pull down', *razrušit'* 'to destroy'), movement (*obojti* 'to walk around', *podnjat'sja* 'to go up') and mental activity (*podumat'* 'to think', *ponimat'* 'to understand', *sčitat'* 'to suggest').

Interestingly, the proportion of nouns and verbs in the keyword list from Pribylovskij's translation is the same as in the translation by Task, but the numbers are smaller. The keyword lists show therefore that both Pribylovskij's and Task's translations are more 'static' than other translations, that is, they pay more attention to objects than to actions.

4 Conclusions

The corpus-based analysis of the six translations of Orwell's *Animal Farm* made it possible to detect relations between different translation, measure the distances between them and even find some peculiarities of individual translations.

The frequency-list-based comparison of the texts proved to be very efficient, and the multidimensional scaling method makes it possible to visualise relations between the texts. Using a machine translation of the source text as a 'starting point' seems to work well; it may be an alternative to a literal translation. The poor quality of MT may skew, to some extent, the results. Still, using one of human translations for the purpose would be much worse.

The keyword analysis gives additional data to the research, and it confirms the findings of the MDS analysis. It also makes it possible to find lexical classes, parts of speech or certain lexemes that may yield additional data. The study of keyword lists and the statistics drawn from these helps a researcher to get an idea what to look for.

The most interesting result of this mini-research is that, at least in this concrete case, the first translation was not the most domesticated, as it should be according to the retranslation hypothesis. The first translation was the most literal and the closest to the original text. The later translations are less literal and pursue readability and naturalness of the language of translation. The publishers tend to choose for publishing the translations that are written in more natural language, and this (sadly) means that the faithfulness to the original and the quest for giving the most exact picture of the original work does not interest the publishers and, most likely, neither the readers.

What is important is that the methods presented in this chapter are applicable not only to prose; they work with translations of poetry and drama as well. The results of the analysis of concrete empirical data can also aid in the fields of language technologies, plagiarism detection and other disciplines that study similarities in texts.

The development of corpus-based methods to study retranslations can be of great use for translation studies in that they offer quantitative measures for comparing translations and their quality evaluation. It becomes possible to manage very large sets of data, to study large works that were translated many times.

In this particular study, the alignments were used for concordancing purposes only. The distance measure and keyword searches could have been performed on unaligned texts as well. However, possessing aligned parallel texts opens many other possibilities for research and for comparing parallel texts: omissions or additions can be discovered, use of certain translation equivalents can be mapped, etc. Indeed, a large parallel corpus of retranslations aligned on sentence or even on word level would be of great use. Sadly, aligning multiple translations is still very difficult technically. The standard aligning software was not developed for such ambitious tasks; they are made for aligning pairs of technical manuals, agreements or other documents written in standardised language and with clear structure. Aligning literary texts is much more difficult, even pairwise. It was possible to align eight parallel texts of *Animal Farm* with LF Aligner for this study, but aligning 40 translations of one fragment from *Macbeth* in the Tom Cheesman's project was a very demanding task (see Cheesman et al., 2017, p. 744). Huge parallel corpora of the Bible became technically possible only because the verses of the Bible are numbered, and thus the aligning had been already performed manually a long time ago and by other people.

Notes

1 The analysis could have been done with the *stylo* package for R (Eder et al., 2016), but the package does not have special support for Russian. The processing would have been done without lemmatisation. For this reason it was decided to process lemmatised word lists generated from the corpus with TextHammer using R packages for cluster analysis and multidimensional scaling.
2 It would have been possible to use absolute frequencies, since the texts are translations of the same source text and do not differ much in length. However, normalised frequencies give a better picture.

References

Alharbi, M., Laramee, R. S., & Cheesman, T. (2015). TransVis: Integrated distant and close reading of Othello translations. *Journal of Latex Class Files, 14*(8), 1–18. https://doi.org/10.1109/TVCG.2020.3012778

Brownlie, S. (2006). Narrative theory and retranslation theory. *Across Languages and Cultures, 7*(2), 145–170.

Cadera, S. M., & Walsh, A. S. (Eds.). (2017). *Literary retranslation in context.* New Trends in Translation Studies. Oxford, Bern, Berlin, Bruxelles, Frankfurt am Main, New York, Wien: Peter Lang.

Čermakova, A., & Farova, L. (2010). Keywords in Harry Potter and their Czech and Finnish translation equivalents. In F. Čermak, et al. (Eds.), *InterCorp: Exploring a multilingual corpus* (pp. 177–188). Prague: Nakladatelství Lidové Noviny/ Czech National Corpus.

Cheesman, T., Flanagan, K., Thiel, S., Rybicki, J., Laramee, R. S., Hope, J., & Roos, A. (2017). Multi-retranslation corpora: Visibility, variation, value, and virtue. *Digital Scholarship in the Humanities, 32*(4), 739–760. https://doi.org/10.1093/llc/fqw027

Deane-Cox, S. (2014). *Retranslation: Literature and reinterpretation.* London: Bloomsbury.

Desmidt, I. (2009). (Re)translation revisited. *Meta, 54*(4), 669–683.

Eder, M., Rybicki, J., & Kestemont, M. (2016). Stylometry with R: A package for computational text analysis. *The R Journal, 16*(1), 107–121. https://journal.r-project.org/archive/2016/RJ-2016-007/RJ-2016-007.pdf

FantLab (n.d.) Džordž Oruèll. Skotnyj dvor. *FantLab, Laboratorija Fantastiki.* https://fantlab.ru/work9633

Fidler, M., & Cvrček, V. (2015). A data-driven analysis of reader viewpoints: Reconstructing the historical reader using keyword analysis. *Journal of Slavic Linguistics, 23*(2), 197–239.

Johnson, S., & Esslin, A. (2006). Language in the news: Some reflections on keyword analysis using Wordsmith Tools and the BNC. *Leeds Working Papers in Linguistics, #11.* www.leeds.ac.uk/arts/info/125154/leeds_working_papers_in_ linguistics_and_phonetics/1949/volume_11_2006

Jones, H. (2020). Retranslating Thucydides as a scientific historian: A corpus-based analysis. *Target, 32*(1), 59–82. doi.org/10.1075/target.19082.jon

Kemppanen, H. (2004). Keywords and ideology in translated history texts: A corpus-based analysis. *Across Languages and Cultures, 5*(1), 89–106.

Kemppanen, H. (2008). *Avainsanoja ja ideologiaa: käännettyjen ja ei-käännettyjen historiatekstien korpuslingvistinen analyysi.* Joensuu: University of Joensuu.

Kilgarriff, A. (1997). Using word frequency lists to measure corpus homogeneity and similarity between corpora. *Information Technology Research Institute.* Technical Report Series. 97–07. http://aclweb.org/anthology/W97-0122

Kilgarriff, A. (2001). Comparing corpora. *International Journal of Corpus Linguistics, 6*(1), 97–133. www.sketchengine.eu/wp-content/uploads/comparing_ corpora_2001.pdf

Kilgarriff, A. (2009). Simple maths for keywords. In M. Mahlberg, et al. (Eds.), *Proceedings of corpus linguistics conference CL2009.* UK: University of Liverpool.

www.sketchengine.eu/wp-content/uploads/2015/04/2009-Simple-maths-for-keywords.pdf

Koskinen, K., & Paloposki, O. (2015). *Sata kirjaa, tuhat suomennosta: Kaunokirjallisuuden uudelleenkääntäminen*. Helsinki: SKS.

Kuusi, P. (2014). Kääntämisen universaaleja uudelleenkäännöksissä. *MikaEL, 4*. https://sktl-fi-bin.directo.fi/@Bin/0ee65f8d4916a5370ceb8374ebf00d7e/1419945515/application/pdf/533414/Kuusi_MikaEL2014.pdf

Ljaševskaja, O. N., & Šarov, S. A. (2009). *Častotnyj slovar' sovremennogo russkogo jazyka* (na materialah Nacional'nogo korpusa russkogo jazyka). Moskva: Azbukovnik. http://dict.ruslang.ru

Mayer, T., & Cysouw, M. (2014). Creating a massively parallel bible corpus. In *LREC 2014, ninth international conference on language resources and evaluation* (pp. 3158–3163), Reykjavik, Iceland. www.lrec-conf.org/proceedings/lrec2014/pdf/220_Paper.pdf

McCarthy, A., Wicks, R., Lewis, D., Mueller, A., Wu, W., Adams, O., Nicolai, G., Post, M., & Yarowsky, D. (2020). The Johns Hopkins University bible corpus: 1600+ tongues for typological exploration. In *Proceedings of the 12th language resources and evaluation conference* (pp. 2884–2892), Marceille, France. www.aclweb.org/anthology/2020.lrec-1.352.pdf

Milizia, D. (2010). Keywords and phrases in political speeches. In M. Bondi & M. Scott (Eds.), *Keyness in text* (pp. 127–145). Amsterdam & Philadelphia: John Benjamins.

Mikhailov, M. (2019). The extent of similarity: Comparing texts by their frequency lists. In Jantunen, J. H. et al. (Eds.), *Proceedings of the research data and humanities (RDHum) 2019 Conference: Data, methods and tools*. Oulu: University of Oulu, pp. 159–178. (Studia humaniora ouluensia 17).

Mikhailov, M., & Cooper, R. (2016). *Corpus linguistics for translation and contrastive studies: A guide for research*. London and New York: Routledge.

Munday, J. (1998). A computer-assisted approach to the analysis of translation shifts. *Meta, 43*(4), 542–556.

Nida, E. A., & Taber, C. R. (1974). *The theory and practice of translation*. Leiden: Published for the United Bible Societies by E.J. Brill.

Paloposki, O., & Koskinen, S. K. (2010). Reprocessing texts: The fine line between retranslating and revising. *Across Languages and Cultures, 11*(1), 29–49.

Piperski, A. (2017). Sravnenie korpusov meroj χ^2: simvoly, slova, lemmy ili časterečnye pomety? [Comparing corpora with χ^2: Characters, words, lemmata, or PoS tags?]. In *Korpusnaja lingvistika – 2017* [Corpus linguistics–2017] (pp. 282–286). Saint Petersburg: Saint Petersburg State University.

Piperski, A. (2018, May 30–June 2). Corpus size and the robustness of measures of corpus distance. In *Computational linguistics and intellectual technologies: Proceedings of the international conference "dialogue 2018"*, Moscow. www.dialog-21.ru/media/4327/piperskiach.pdf

Pouke van, P., & Gallego, G. S. (2019). Retranslation in context. *Cadernos de Tradução, 39*(1), 10–22.

Scott, M., & Tribble, C. (2006). *Textual patterns: Key words and corpus analysis in language education*. Amsterdam: John Benjamins.

Seale, C., Charteris-Black, J., & Ziebland, S. (2006). Gender, cancer experience and internet use: A comparative keyword analysis of interviews and online cancer support groups. *Social Science and Medicine*, *62*(10), 2577–2590.

Venuti, L. (1995). *The translator's invisibility: A history of translation*. London & New York: Routledge.

Wilkinson, M. (2014). Using the keyword tool to explore lexical differences between British and American English in specialised corpora. *CALL-EJ*, *15*(1), 21–38. http://callej.org/journal/15-1/Wilkinson_2014.pdf

Appendix

Research data

Orwell: Orwell, George. *Animal Farm*, 1945.
Bespalova: Оруэлл, Джордж. *Скотный двор*. Пер. с англ. Беспалова, Лариса, 1989.
Kibirskij: Оруэлл, Джордж. *Ферма животных*. Пер. с англ. Кибирский С., 1989.
Polotsk: Оруэлл, Джордж. *Скотский хутор*. Пер. с англ. Полоцк, Илан, 1989.
Task: Оруэлл, Джордж. *Скотский уголок*. Пер. с англ. Таск, Сергей, 1988.
Pribylovskij: Оруэлл, Джордж. *Ферма животных*. Пер. с англ. Прибыловский В., 1986.
Struve and Kriger: Оруэлл, Джордж. *Скотский хутор*. Пер. с англ. Струве, Глеб и Кригер, Марина, 1949.

4 Exploring semantic annotations to measure post-editing quality

Felipe Almeida Costa, Thiago Castro Ferreira, Adriana Silvina Pagano, and Wagner Meira, Jr.

1 Introduction

Machine-translation performance has grown exponentially in recent years, closely matching or even outperforming human translators in some language pairs, as can be seen in the findings of the 2019 Conference on Machine Translation (WMT19) (Barrault et al., 2019). To the extent that its output is increasingly adequate and fluent, the question arises as to the part human translators have in the shared labor of this process. In this sense, a very productive research theme to explore machine–human cooperation is human post-editing of automatically machine-translated texts, particularly in terms of post editing effort and quality. This is done based on variables such as time (Specia, 2011; Cumbreño & Aranberri, 2019), editing distance (Specia & Farzindar, 2010), source text characteristics (Tatsumi & Routurier, 2010), post-editor profile (Green et al., 2013; De Almeida, 2013) and perceived effort as reported by post-editors (Koponen, 2012).

One particular strand of research meriting attention is the relation between post-editing effort and quality of post-edited texts. Vieira (2017) argues that the latter has been dealt with mostly for the purposes of comparing post-editing with traditional translation workflows and proposes adding more variables into the connection effort-quality. He, for one, pursues process-oriented measures of post-editing effort. Triangulated with product measures, post-editing behavior can provide insights into how effort can predict quality both in terms of fluency and adequacy to text standards.

Whereas Vieira probes individual traits and post-editor behavior in search for predictors of post-edited quality, our research seeks to explore a further variable that, to the best of our knowledge, has not been hitherto investigated: conceptual text complexity. Drawing on Štajner and Hulpus (2018), we approach conceptual text complexity on the premise that semantic relations implicated in the meanings construed in a text add to its complexity, which can be computed on the basis of the number of predicates in a text. Complementary measures of complexity posited in the literature are

DOI: 10.4324/9781003102694-4

semantic domain, number of sentences and number of pronouns as indicators of coreferentiality in discourse.

To explore this new variable, we collected a corpus of English–Portuguese post-edited translations aligned with structured semantic annotations. As input to our study, we used English texts retrieved from WebNLG (Colin et al., 2016; Gardent et al., 2017a, 2017b), a semantically annotated corpus consisting of English texts of different content size (one to seven properties), aligned with their semantic representations (Resource Description Framework – RDF), labelled according to 15 semantic categories. After automatically translating the selected texts from English into Brazilian Portuguese by means of a popular commercial machine translation engine, a web interface was developed so that recruited translation students could post-edit the automatically translated texts. These participants could perform the task in two different modes according to their preference: a free-editing mode or a guided mode with four word-level operations (insertion to the right, insertion to the left, deletion and substitution).

Upon collecting our corpus, we carried out a study on the language pair English–Brazilian Portuguese, with the overall aim of investigating contributing factors to post-editing quality purporting to answer the following question: Does conceptual text complexity explain the quality of a post-edited translation? In complementarity to our main research question, we also addressed two of the main issues regarding post-editing in machine-translation workflows: Does quality of machine-translation output play a major role in post-editing quality? If so, and given the recent advances in machine translation, is post-editing a worthwhile operation at all?

To answer our research questions, we developed a linear regression to account for quality of post-editing based on semantic category of text and number of semantic relationships, including as additional factors number of sentences, pronominal coreference, quality of the raw machine-translation output and post-editing effort.

The remainder of this chapter is organized as follows: Section 2 briefly provides a background to the motivation of our study. Section 3 details how we obtained the corpus of our study. Section 4 presents the variables pursued in our study. In Section 5 we discuss and interpret the output of the interpretable model by indicating significant variables and how each variable impacts post-editing quality. Section 6 summarizes our work and main findings, followed by our suggestions to further expand it. The source texts, the automatic and post-edited translations and the findings of our analysis are publicly available in our repository.[1]

2 Motivation

Post-editing is largely acknowledged as a task meant to fix up the output of a machine-translation system, be that carried out by a human or automatically. When human post-editing is used, the whole operation is also referred to as computer-aided human translation as opposed to automatic machine translation.

Post-editing of machine translation has been appealing for both engineers and translators. For the former group, the task allows the rapid and cheap customization of general-purpose machine-translation models to specific application domains, avoiding the need for new systems to be trained from scratch (Correia & Martins, 2019; Costa et al., 2020). For translators, post-editing of machine-translation output is assumed to be faster and implicate less effort than translating from scratch.

Most studies on post-editing tackle the key issues of quality and effort. Human post-editing has been the target of a large body of research, particularly regarding the amount and nature of effort invested by humans in the task and the kind of insights studies can bring both into human translator training and applications for machine translation and automatic post-editing.

In particular, studies on human post-editing effort have been pursued focusing on the temporal, cognitive and technical aspects of the task (Krings, 2001). Temporal effort is measured based on time spent by humans to post-edit MT output. Cognitive aspects have been posited to linguistic choices made by post-editors. Technical aspects are measured by the number of editing operations (insertions, deletions and shifts) performed to obtain the post-edited version.

Editing operations have allowed a number of metrics to evaluate post-editing effort. One such metric is TER, which measures the distance between machine translations and their post-edited versions. The more distant post-edited versions are, the more effort is assumed to have been invested in improving machine-translation output.

Post-editing effort is a relevant measure to evaluate machine-translation quality in computer-aided human translation workflows. Among the factors that have been investigated pertaining to source text characteristics are sentence length, syntactic structure, count and distribution of different parts of speech and particular linguistic constructions (Vieira, 2014; Green et al., 2013; O'Brien, 2011; Tatsumi & Roturier, 2010; Aziz et al., 2014). Sentence length has been found to be a relevant factor in that longer sentences demand more cognitive effort to post-edit (Koponen, 2012), despite the fact that sentence length does not necessarily correlate with post-editing time (Aziz et al., 2014). Sub-sentential segments involving distinct linguistic patterns, such as modal verbs, adverbs and coordinating conjunctions, have also been suggested as triggers of more post-editing effort (Aziz et al., 2014). Although features like these have been targeted in previous studies, we are not aware, to the best of our knowledge, of any study that has looked into how conceptual text complexity impacts post-editing effort. To explore conceptual text complexity as a factor in post-editing quality, we collected a

86 *Felipe Almeida Costa et al.*

corpus of English–Portuguese post-edited translations in which each one of them is linked to a structured meaning representation of its content. Details on corpus compilation are provided in the following section.

3 Data gathering

In this section we describe the rationale and procedures we followed to collect our corpus of post-edited texts, first reported in Costa et al. (2020).

3.1 Source data

The source English texts in our corpus were extracted from the WebNLG corpus (Colin et al., 2016; Gardent et al., 2017a). This data set consists of paired instances between a meaning representation and its English verbalization. It was initially built for the natural language process task of data-to-text generation, that is, automatically verbalizing a meaning representation.

The WebNLG corpus was particularly suitable for our purposes, as it allowed us to explore conceptual text complexity, that is, the amount of information that has to be processed by the post-editor in order to understand the source text and make decisions to post-edit it. The corpus was compiled on the basis of semantic representations as expressed by means of structures. These structures are part of the Resource Description Framework (RDF) developed by the World Wide Web Consortium (W3C) in order to enable machine processing of information. Within RDF, information is structured as statements made up by a Subject, a Property and an Object. The assumption is that things in the world enter relations defined by properties, and these in turn have values. For instance, a relationship between a human being and a location can be one of "place of birth". This can be formulated as Subject (Person) has as place of birth (Property) a location (Object), as illustrated by the following structure retrieved from our corpus in Table 4.1:

Table 4.1 Example of an RDF structure

Subject	Property	Object
Aleksander_Barkov,_Jr.	birthPlace	Tampere, Finland

Structures as that shown in Table 4.1 are also referred to as "triples" and consist of

- the thing the statement describes (Person "Aleksander_Barkov,_Jr.");
- a specific property ("birthPlace") of the thing the statement describes;

- the thing the statement says is the value of the property (the birthplace location "Tampere, Finland").

To express more complex relations, sets of multiple RDF triples are used, implicating more properties. Figure 4.1 illustrates four triples, which can be combined to yield verbalizations such as those shown for our example.

Figure 4.1 shows an example of a WebNLG paired instance between a meaning representation and its English verbalizations. In this representation, each property determines a transitive relation between the subject and the object. In Figure 4.1, for instance, a property such as "birth year" establishes a relation between the subject "Aleksander Barkov Jr." and "1995", indicating the year that the subject was born.

The fact that the WebNLG corpus is made up of meaning representations and their corresponding verbalizations allows us to investigate conceptual text complexity as estimated by the number of semantic relations that are implicated in a given text. It is assumed that the higher the number of properties, the more complex the meaning construed. In this sense, number of properties can be taken as a measure of conceptual text complexity (Štajner & Hulpus, 2018).

The WebNLG corpus compiles verbalizations of meaning representations (i.e. sets of triples), which were collected in an experiment with human participants recruited from a crowdsourcing platform (Gardent et al., 2017a).

Subject	Property	Object
Aleksander_Barkov,_Jr.	birthYear	1995
Aleksander_Barkov,_Jr.	position	Center_(ice_hockey)
Aleksander_Barkov,_Jr.	club	Florida_Panthers
Aleksander_Barkov,_Jr.	birthPlace	Tampere, Finland

↓

Verbalization 1	Aleksander Barkov Jr, a center for the Florida Panthers, was born 1995 in Tampere, Finland.
Verbalization 2	Aleksander Barkov, Jr. was born in 1995, in Tampere, Finland. His ice hockey position is center, and his club is the Florida Panthers.
Verbalization 3	Aleksander Barkov Jr was born in Tampere, Finland in 1995. He plays as a center for the Florida Panthers.

Figure 4.1 Example of a single instance in the WebNLG corpus.

The participants were instructed to provide coherent descriptions of all the triples by means of clauses and clause complexes combined in such a way that no two verbalizations were identical.

Concerning size, the WebNLG corpus has a total 42,901 English texts describing 16,095 sets of triples, an average of 2.67 verbalizations per set. For evaluation purposes, the paired sets of triples and their verbalizations are distributed into training (34,536), development (4,217) and test (4,841) sets. Aiming to decrease redundancy, their distribution builds on a constrained strategy, that is, the triple set of inputs on the test set should have no overlap with the triple set of inputs on the training and development sets (Shimorina & Gardent, 2018). The verbalizations cover 15 semantic categories, namely: Airport, Artist, Astronaut, Athlete, Building, Celestial Body, City, Comics Character, Food, Means Of Transportation, Monument, Politician, Sports Team, University, and Written Work.

For our study, we extracted the test partition of the corpus to be machine translated and the output post edited by human annotators. This set contains 4,148 verbalizations produced on the input of 1 to 5 RDF triples. The categories Astronaut and Monument do not occur in the test set.

3.2 Machine-translated outputs

English verbalizations were automatically translated into Portuguese using the DeepL Translator, an increasingly popular neural MT application in industry. DeepL's superior performance over similar MT tools accounts for its selection, even though it would allow us to obtain translations into European Portuguese and not Brazilian Portuguese, our intended target language for the experiment.[2]

Like other novel translation tools, DeepL Translator is built based on neural machine translation (NMT). Neural machine translation models have outperformed statistical models in fluency (Tu et al., 2016). In general, these models make use of neural networks and work by producing a vector representation of the input sentence, which is later word-by-word converted into the most likely translation. Although they require more data and time to be developed, NMT models can better generalize the patterns in the language, consequently outputting a better translation.

3.3 Human post-edits

To obtain the human post-edits, we designed a web interface for this study.[3] As depicted in Figures 4.2 and 4.3, participants are presented with the original text, a label for its domain category and the machine-translation output. They may either edit the machine translation from a text-box (so-called *free*

Measuring post-editing quality 89

Figure 4.2 Screenshot of free mode PE system developed for data collection

mode – Figure 4.2) or on a *guided mode*, where a set of operations may be used to post-edit the translation (Figure 4.3). The operations were defined based on neural programmer-interpreter approaches for APE (Vu & Haffari, 2018) and consisted in *insertion to the right*, *insertion to the left*, *delete* and *update*.

In Figure 4.2, a screenshot of the PE system developed for our study shows the tool in its free mode. The top bar shows the annotator's login, his/her annotation count, time elapsed since login, and pause and exit buttons. Below is the tool's mode type selector (either free or guided), semantic category for input text (airport), the English source text and a text-box containing the machine-translation output. Below the text-box, the button on the left ("Pular") allows the annotator to skip the current source text, if he or she feels unable to post-edit; the button on the right ("Confirmar tradução") allows the annotator to submit his/her annotation after he/she is done with his/her post-editing.

Figure 4.3 shows a screenshot of our PE system in its guided mode. The interface is similar to the one in free mode, except for the machine output being presented as regular text and predefined post-editing operations appearing to the annotator when hovering over words.

Prior to post-editing, participants received instructions requesting them (1) to transliterate entity names whenever transliteration was available; (2) not to pause the post-editing session while consulting external sources; and (3) to adapt the machine output to Brazilian Portuguese whenever necessary.

90 Felipe Almeida Costa et al.

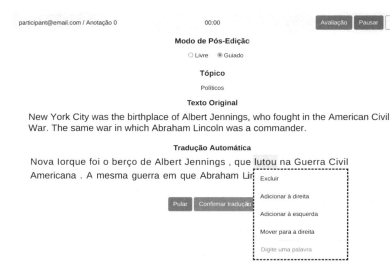

Figure 4.3 Screenshot of guided mode PE system developed for data collection

In total, we recruited a group of 37 participants to post-edit the machine-translated texts. Portuguese was their L1 and English their L2. Thirty-three of them reported an upper-intermediate proficiency level of English, while four reported an intermediate one. In order to prevent human errors and human biases, each machine-translation output was post-edited by two independent participants.

Our postediting tool measured the time spent on each verbalization, pausing time, the operations and their order in guided mode, log of intermediate editions in free mode and skipped verbalizations. For the present study, however, we have concentrated mostly on the verbalizations metadata, which include its category, triple set size and extracted features from the verbalization. We have also considered the machine output quality obtained during the evaluation task described in section 3.4 and the post-editing effort measured by the TER between the machine output and the human post-edition. Data such as time, pausing time and number of skips will be addressed in future works.

3.4 Quality assurance

In order to check the quality of translated texts (both machine and human), we carried out a task in which a third participant was asked to evaluate them as

Figure 4.4 Screenshot of evaluation system developed for data collection

well as the machine-translated output on a scale ranging from very poor, poor, medium and good to very good. All versions – machine translated and post-edited – were presented on a single screen with no indication of their status, so that the participant could weigh all versions at the same time and with no prior knowledge regarding whether they were machine or human output. Figure 4.4 shows a screenshot of the evaluation system developed for our study.

Our evaluation system, shown in Figure 4.4, presents post-edited texts alongside with the raw machine-translated text, randomly sorted and labeled as numbered candidate texts in order to avoid annotator's bias. Whenever two post-edited texts were identical to each other or one or two of them were identical to the machine-translated text, only a single instance was shown to the evaluator. Figure 4.4 shows an example where the evaluator has to assess two candidate texts. In this particular case, one of the post-edited texts was identical to the raw machine output.

Having machine-translated texts together with post-edited texts allowed us to obtain an evaluation for them, which was instrumental to include raw machine-translation output as a variable in our analysis.

3.5 Final corpus

In total, we obtained 8,296 post-edited texts (two post-edited versions per source text) evaluated by the quality assurance procedure described in the previous section. Table 4.2 depicts the distribution of the post-edited translations per semantic category and size of the triple set.

92 *Felipe Almeida Costa et al.*

Table 4.2 Post-edited texts per category and triple set size

Domain/triple set size	1	2	3	4	5	Total
Airport	42	22	0	0	0	64
Artist	8	6	0	0	0	14
Athlete	288	112	114	74	12	600
Building	162	132	104	68	16	482
Celestial Body	276	218	154	170	92	910
City	356	84	124	94	88	746
Comics Character	418	352	260	88	0	1,118
Food	64	38	12	20	2	136
Means of Transportation	242	206	160	134	46	788
Politician	186	138	82	88	32	526
Sports Team	452	358	250	166	16	1,242
University	6	0	0	0	0	6
Written Work	510	476	466	212	0	1,664
ALL	3,010	2,142	1,726	1,114	304	8,296

The distribution of categories in our corpus can be accounted for by the particular design of WebNLG. As mentioned previously, the categories and triple set size are not equally distributed in the WebNLG corpus. This disproportion is extended to its partitions. While some categories such as Sports Teams and City are well distributed and have a considerable number of posteditions, the ones belonging to semantic categories Airport, Artist and University do not amount to more than 1% of the total.

Regarding quality labels assigned to them by our evaluator, our corpus has the following distribution (Figure 4.5).

Figure 4.5 shows the distribution of the post-edited translations per quality mark in a five-point scale comprising the labels very poor, poor, medium, good and very good. This scale was intended to allow a more finegrained evaluation.

From the total number of post-edited texts, those which ranked very poor and poor account for slightly over 7% of our corpus, while texts ranking good and very good represent 76.18%.

The corpus compiled in our study, made up of source texts in English aligned with structured semantic annotations, together with their machine translations and their post-edited versions in Brazilian Portuguese, the latter having quality labels assigned by a human evaluator, is, as far as we know, unique in its kind, and its potential for exploration can be seen in our analysis reported in the following section.

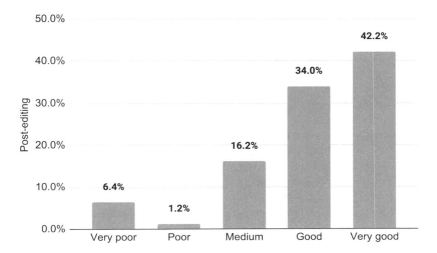

Figure 4.5 Post-editing quality distribution

4 Analysis

The main goal of our study was to investigate contributing factors to post-editing quality, with a special interest in conceptual text complexity. To that end, we run a linear regression to predict the quality of the obtained post-edited texts based on independent variables related to six dimensions: domain of source text, size of the triple set, number of sentences in the source text, number of pronouns in the source text, machine output quality and required post-editing effort.

Semantic category: We were interested in distinguishing those semantic categories where the quality of the post-edited texts were acceptable from the ones that were not. To approach this, we considered the category of the verbalized text provided by the WebNLG, corpus based on the related meaning representation (e.g., Airport, Astronaut, Monument, etc.), as one of the independent variables in our regression.

Text complexity: In order to understand how the complexity of the verbalized text as well as the amount of information it conveyed impact the quality of the post-edited text, we considered the number of triples in the related meaning representation, the number of sentences and the number of pronouns in their verbalization as independent variables. We assumed that the higher the number of triples in the related meaning representation, the more complex the source text is. Number of sentences was also considered a variable, since there are reports in the literature as to its likely impact on post-editing effort. Pronouns were taken as indicators of complexity in terms of co-referential relations. We did not take sentence length into account, as we found it to be redundant with triple set size, since those two correlate with a 0.87 Pearson's coefficient.

Machine-translation quality: We investigated the impact of the quality of the machine-translated text on the quality of the post-edited texts. In other words, we wanted to understand how good the quality of the machine-translated text needed to be for post-editors to perform in such a way as to reach a good quality target text with minimum effort. To represent this dimension, we fed the linear regression with the quality label of the machine-translated text related to the target post-edited text, obtained during the evaluation task previously described in section 3.4.

Post-editing effort: To investigate whether post-editing actually contributes to improving the quality of machine translation, we fed our linear regression with the TER measure as an independent variable. This measure is used to compare a machine-translated text with its post-edited version by measuring distance from the former to the latter in terms of word-level insertion, deletion and update operations. TER ranges between 0 and 1, where 0 means that both texts are identical while 1 means that the machine-translated text and its corresponding post-edited version are completely different.

5 Results and discussion

A linear regression yielded the coefficients and p-values shown in Table 4.3, which explains the impact of semantic category, text complexity, machine-translation quality and post-editing effort on the quality of the corresponding post-edited translation. With these independent variables, our linear regression can explain the quality of post-edits with a 0.387 coefficient of determination (r-squared). In the following sections, we zoom in on each one of these variables.

5.1 Semantic categories

Results about the impact of semantic categories show that the quality of the post-edited texts from the Comics Character category tend to be significantly

Table 4.3 Linear regression output

	Coefficient	p-value
Intercept	2.0132	0.000
Category		
Artist	0.0529	0.835
Athlete	0.0504	0.657
Building	−0.0487	0.672
Celestial Body	−0.1475	0.187
City	−0.0829	0.461
Comics Character	0.2513	**0.023**
Food	−0.3541	**0.007**
Means of Transportation	0.0978	0.384
Politician	0.0938	0.412
Sports Team	0.0132	0.905
University	0.0721	0.845
Written Work	−0.0490	0.656
Text complexity		
Triple set size	−0.0311	**0.001**
Sentence count	−0.0203	0.242
Pronoun (count)	−0.0199	0.516
Machine translation quality	0.5343	**0.000**
Post-editing effort (TER)	1.6758	**0.000**

Table 4.4 Comics character category example

	Text	Quality label
Source	Drake Stevens is known as the comic character Airman.	
Machines Translation	Drake Stevens é conhecido como o personagem de banda desenhada Airman.	very poor
Post-edited	Drake Stevens é conhecido como o personagem de quadrinhos Airman.	good

higher, whereas the ones in the Food category follow the opposite direction, tending to be significantly lower.

In the Comics Character category, we observed that translations obtained by DeepL contained a high number of terms used in European Portuguese, easily spotted and corrected by the recruited post-editors, which led to post-editing having a higher quality label than the machine output. This is shown in the example in Table 4.4.

In Table 4.4, "comic character" is automatically translated as "personagem de banda desenhada", a term that is used in European Portuguese.

Table 4.5 Food category example

	Text	Quality label
Source	Strawberries can be added to barny cakes.	
Machine translation	Os morangos podem ser adicionados aos bolos de cevada.	very poor
Post-edition 1	Morangos podem ser adicionados aos bolos de cevada.	medium
Post-edition 2	Os morangos podem ser adicionados aos bolos de cevada.	very poor

This automatic translation is scored as "very poor" by the evaluator. In both post-edited texts, the European Portuguese term is replaced by its Brazilian Portuguese counterpart, "personagem de quadrinhos", which is rated as "good" by the evaluator. Editings like this account for the scores given to post-edited texts in this semantic category to be good.

Regarding the post-edited translations in the Food category, we ascribe their poor quality to the occurrence of unfamiliar lexical items in the source texts, such as brand names of food or names of typical dishes. These were either left untranslated or mistranslated in the automatically translated texts, as seen in our example In Table 4.5.

"Barny cakes" is a brand name for children's biscuits. The machine has no match for it as a proper noun and translates it as "barley cakes" ("bolos de cevada"). Both post-editors fail to correct this misinterpretation; so does the evaluator, who rates post-editing 1 slightly better due to the post-editor's choice of leaving out the definite article "the" ("os") to make the statement generic in Portuguese.

5.2 Conceptual text complexity

To understand how the complexity of the texts influences the quality of their post-editing, we analyzed the number of triples in verbalizations as well as the number of sentences and the number of pronouns in the source texts.

Linear regression shows that neither the number of sentences nor the number of pronouns has a significant impact on the quality of post-editing. Regarding the number of sentences, some studies in the literature report a correlation between sentence length and editing time, even though this does not necessarily correlate with difficulty in comprehension. In fact, it is not the number of sentences or their length that may add complexity but particular linguistic structures (see Aziz et al., 2014).

Concerning the number of pronouns, our result shows that co-reference did not play a major role in the quality of the post-edited texts. This may be due to the unequivocal relations established by pronouns between sentences in the source texts, which did not pose problems of ambiguous referents. Moreover, most pronouns establishing anaphoric relations of co-reference between sentences appear in subject initial position, which further contributes to their easy and straightforward interpretation. The example in Table 4.6 shows one such example, anaphoric pronoun highlighted in bold.

Table 4.6 shows an inter-sentential co-reference relation established between the pronoun "he", which anaphorically refers to "Republican Abner W. Sibal". The pronoun is in subject initial position in the sentence, which further adds to its straightforward interpretation.

If the number of sentences and pronouns did not show any significant impact on post-editing quality, this is not the case with the number of triples in the corresponding meaning representation. Our linear regression shows that the quality of the post-edited texts significantly decreases as the number of triples increases. This means that it is indeed more difficult to post-edit a piece of text that verbalizes multiple clauses. The example in Table 4.7 shows a text in which five triples were verbalized. Neither of the post-editors managed to improve the machine output, as evidenced by their rating.

Table 4.6 Co-reference pronoun example

	Text	Quality label
Source	Republican Abner W. Sibal was born in Ridgewood, Queens on November 4th, 1921. **He** was a member of the Connecticut Senate from the 26th District and was succeeded by Donald J. Irwin	
Machine translation	O republicano Abner W. Sibal nasceu em Ridgewood, Queens a 4 de Novembro de 1921. **Ele** era um membro do Senado de Connecticut do Distrito 26 e foi sucedido por Donald J. Irwin.	good
Post-edited	O republicano Abner W. Sibal nasceu em Ridgewood, Queens em 4 de novembro de 1921. **Ele** era um membro do Senado de Connecticut no Distrito 26, e foi sucedido por Donald J. Irwin.	good

Table 4.7 Example of low quality achieved after post-editing of a 5 triple-verbalization

	Text	Quality label
Source	United States 26th District, Republican, Connecticut Senate member Abner W. Sibal was succeeded by Marjorie Farmer. He was born 04/11/1921 in Ridgewood, Queens.	
Machine translation	Abner W. Sibal, membro do Senado do 26° Distrito, Republicano e Connecticut dos Estados Unidos, foi sucedido por Marjorie Farmer. Nasceu em 11 / 04 / 1921 em Ridgewood, Queens.	very poor
Post-edited text 1	Abner W. Sibal, membro do Senado do 26° Distrito, Republicano e membro do Senado de Connecticut, foi sucedido por Marjorie Farmer. Nasceu em 11 / 04 / 1921 em Ridgewood, Queens.	very poor
Post-edited text 2	Parte do 26° distrito do Senado dos Estados Unidos, republicano, o senador do Connecticut Abner W. Sibal foi sucedido por Marjorie Farmer. Ele nasceu em 04 / 11 / 1921 em Ridgewood, Queens.	very poor

The example in Table 4.7 is an interesting case of a semantic representation implicating a high number of triples. Five properties are verbalized in two sentences, as represented in Table 4.8:

Table 4.8 Triple set for verbalization

Subject	Property	Object
Abner_W._Sibal	office	Member of the Connecticut Senate from the 26th District
Abner_W._Sibal	party	Republican_Party_(United_States)
Abner_W._Sibal	successor	Marjorie_Farmer
Abner_W._Sibal	birthPlace	Ridgewood,_Queens
Abner_W._Sibal	birthDate	1921–04–11

This example shows that a dense semantic representation, involving five distinct properties, may be packed in a low number of sentences (two in this case).

5.3 Machine-output quality

We noticed that the higher the quality of the machine-translation output, the higher the quality of the post-edited texts. As shown in Table 4.3, this independent variable had the second largest coefficient among all the independent variables. This is an important indicator that, to some extent, the quality of the automatic translation a post-editor receives as input may affect his/her work.

Table 4.9 depicts the confusion matrix between the quality of a machine-translated text and its post-edited counterparts. In this table, we can see, for instance, that 184 machine-translated texts which were rated "very poor" had their post-edited versions rated "very good". An example is shown in Table 4.10.

Table 4.9 also shows that there are 11 machine-translated texts that were rated as "very good", their post-edited versions being rated "very poor". The example in Table 4.11 presents one such case.

Table 4.9 Post-editing (PE) quality and machine translation (MT) confusion matrix

MT/PE quality	very poor	poor	medium	good	very good
very poor	345	5	214	258	184
poor	62	90	52	44	64
medium	80	5	846	526	519
good	33	2	175	1833	687
very good	11	0	56	160	2045

Table 4.10 Post-edited text rated higher than its machine-translated counterpart

	Text	Quality label
Source	388 is the number of pages A severed Wasp has.	
Machine translation	388 é o número de páginas que uma vespa cortada tem.	very poor
Post-edited	O livro "A Severed Wasp" tem 388 páginas.	very good

Table 4.11 Post-edited text rated lower than its machine-translated counterpart

	Text	Quality label
Source	Alexandria in Indiana occupies 6.81 square kilometers.	
Machine translation	Alexandria, em Indiana, ocupa 6,81 quilômetros quadrados.	very good
Post-edited	Alexandria, na Índia, ocupa 6,81 quilômetros quadrados.	very poor

5.4 Post-editing effort

Our linear regression shows that the more distant the post-edited text from its machine-translated counterpart, the better is the quality of the former. In other words, this result shows that the post-editing effort significantly improves the quality of the text. In fact, the TER measure was the independent variable with the highest coefficient in the linear regression (e.g., 1.68). A high TER is an indicator of post-editing effort, and several features have been used to explain it in the literature. Aziz et al. (2014) have pointed to the need to carry out more fine-grained explorations of TER, particularly in connection with distinct types of edits. Our results suggest that high conceptual text complexity, as captured by the number of semantic relations, could be an indicator to explain instances of high post-editing.

6 Conclusion

Our study sought to investigate whether the quality of a post-edited text can be explained by its conceptual text complexity as well as additional factors such as the semantic category, quality of the corresponding machine-translation output and post-editing effort. To this end, we first collected a corpus of English–Portuguese post-edited translations, where each post-edited text as well as its corresponding machine translation were annotated according to their quality. Moreover, each pair of machine-translated text and its post-edited version were also attached to a structured representation of their meaning, which allowed us to investigate the quality of post-edits based on factors hitherto unexplored, such as the semantic category of a post-edited translation as well as its conceptual complexity.

To answer our research questions, we developed a linear regression to account for quality of post-editings, taking into account the semantic category, the quality of the raw machine-translation output, the post-editing effort and the number of clauses it verbalizes, as well as the number of sentences and pronominal coreference in the source text.

Our main research question probed the impact of conceptual text complexity on the quality of the post-edited texts. This complexity was represented in the linear regression by the number of predicates verbalized as well as the number of sentences and pronouns in the source text. Results showed that neither the number of sentences of the source text nor the number of pronominal coreferences influence the post-edited quality. On the other hand, the number of predicates verbalized in the texts had a significant negative impact on the quality of the post-edited texts. A likely explanation for this is the fact that a high number of pronouns or sentences does not necessarily entail complexity, whereas a high number of semantic relations does.

Regarding semantic category, at a significance level below 0.05, only Comics Character and Food categories had a significant impact on the post-editing quality in our corpus. While post-edited translations in the Comics Character are likely to have a high quality; the ones from the Food category show a tendency to have low quality. In the former semantic category, we hypothesize that native Brazilian post-editors replaced European Portuguese terms by their Brazilian counterparts, positively impacting the quality of the final text. Moreover, we assumed that the latter domain is a difficult one due to the high frequency of unfamiliar lexical items in the source texts, such as brand names of food or names of typical dishes, which are unknown both to machine-translation systems and human post-editors.

Finally, the results of the linear regression show that the quality of the machine translation and the post-editing effort, represented by the TER measure, were the independent variables that most positively impacted the quality of the post-edited translation. From this pattern, we conclude that post-editing of machine-translated texts is still a much-needed and productive task despite the latest progress in machine-translation state-of-the-art. Complimentarily, the quality of the machine-translation output given as input to the post-editor is crucial to determine whether the final (post-edited) text will have a good quality or not.

Our results suggest that conceptual text complexity, as measured by the number of semantic relations verbalized in the text, is a productive indicator worth pursuing to explain high TER. In that respect, further research including other variables extracted from the annotations, such as which properties of triples are associated with higher post-editing, are expected to shed more light into text complexity, post-editing effort and quality. As to the limitations of our study, some of the variables tracked in the post-editing process, such as task time and pausing time, have not been explored in our regression model. We aim to explore their role in the quality of our post-edited translations in future work.

A relevant product of our study is our corpus compilation, which, as aforementioned, is unique in that it comprises source texts in English aligned with structured semantic annotations, each text being matched to its machine translated output and its post-edited versions in Brazilian Portuguese. The corpus also has quality labels given by a human evaluator to the raw machine-translation output and post-edited versions.

Finally, our approach allows future studies aimed to detect which machine-translated texts demand post-editing from those that have reached sufficient adequacy at the machine output. This is meant to speed up the translation workflow as well as save post-editors' time and effort. Far from removing the human from the workflow, it would mean leveraging human resources in a more productive and efficient manner.

Notes

1 https://github.com/felipealco/webnlg-pt/. Brazilian-Portuguese WebNLG repository.
2 At the time this study was being conducted, Brazilian Portuguese was not among the languages catered for by DeepL, only becoming available on April 2, 2020.
3 Publicly available in playground mode at http://dcc.ufmg.br/~felipealco/webnlg-pt.

Acknowledgments

This research was partially funded by the Brazilian agencies CNPq, CAPES, and FAPEMIG. In particular, the researchers were supported by CNPQ grant No. 310630/2017-7, CAPES Post-doctoral grant No. 88887.508597/2020-00, and FAPEMIG grant APQ-01.461-14. This work was also supported by projects MASWeb, EUBra-BIGSEA, INCT-CYBER, and ATMOSPHERE. We would also wish to express our gratitude to Deepl for kindly granting a license to translate our corpus.

References

Aziz, W., Koponen, M., & Specia, L. (2014). Sub-sentence level analysis of machine translation post-editing effort. In S. O'Brien, L. Winther Balling, M. Carl, M. Simard, & L. Specia (Eds.), *Post-editing of machine translation: Processes and applications* (pp. 170–199). Newcastle upon Tyne, UK: Cambridge Scholars Publishing.

Barrault, L., Bojar, O., Costa-Jussà, M. R., Federmann, C., Fishel, M., Graham, Y., ... Zampieri, M. (2019, August). Findings of the 2019 conference on machine translation (wmt19). In *Proceedings of the fourth conference on machine translation* (Vol. 2: Shared Task Papers, Day 1) (pp. 1–61). Stroudsburg, PA: Association for Computational Linguistics.

Colin, E., Gardent, C., M'rabet, Y., Narayan, S., & Perez-Beltrachini, L. (2016). The WebNLG challenge: Generating text from DBPedia data. In *Proceedings of the 9th international natural language generation conference* (pp. 163–167). Stroudsburg, PA: Association for Computational Linguistics.

Correia, G. M., & Martins, A. F. (2019). A simple and effective approach to automatic post-editing with transfer learning. In *Proceedings of the 57th Annual Meeting of the Association for Computational Linguistics* (pp. 3050–3056). Stroudsburg, PA: Association for Computational Linguistics.

Costa, F. A., Ferreira, T. C., Pagano, A., & Meira, W. (2020). Building the first English-Brazilian Portuguese corpus for automatic post-editing. In *Proceedings of the 28th international conference on computational linguistics* (pp. 6063–6069). International Committee on Computational Linguistics.

Cumbreño, C., & Aranberri, N. (2019). Comparison of temporal, technical and cognitive dimension measurements for post-editing effort. In *Proceedings of the second MEMENTO workshop on modelling parameters of cognitive effort in translation production* (pp. 5–6). Switzerland: European Association for Machine Translation.

De Almeida, G. (2013). *Translating the post-editor: An investigation of post-editing changes and correlations with professional experience across two Romance languages* (Doctoral dissertation). Dublin City University.

Gardent, C., Shimorina, A., Narayan, S., & Perez-Beltrachini, L. (2017a). Creating training corpora for NLG micro-planning. In *55th annual meeting of the Association for Computational Linguistics (ACL)* (pp 179–188). Stroudsburg, PA: Association for Computational Linguistics.

Gardent, C., Shimorina, A., Narayan, S., & Perez-Beltrachini, L. (2017b). The WebNLG challenge: Generating text from RDF data. In *Proceedings of the 10th international conference on natural language generation* (pp. 124–133). Stroudsburg, PA: Association for Computational Linguistics.

Green, S., Heer, J., & Manning, C. D. (2013, April). The efficacy of human post-editing for language translation. In *Proceedings of the SIGCHI conference on human factors in computing systems* (pp. 439–448). New York, NY: Association for Computing Machinery.

Koponen, M. (2012, June). Comparing human perceptions of post-editing effort with post-editing operations. In *Proceedings of the seventh workshop on statistical machine translation* (pp. 181–190). Stroudsburg, PA: Association for Computational Linguistics.

Krings, H. P. (2001). *Repairing texts: Empirical investigations of machine translation post-editing processes* (Vol. 5). Kent, OH: Kent State University Press.

O'Brien, S. (2011). Towards predicting post-editing productivity. *Machine Translation*, *25*(3), 197. Dordrecht: Springer Netherlands.

Shimorina, A., & Gardent, C. (2018, November). Handling rare items in data-to-text generation. In *Proceedings of the 11th international conference on natural language generation* (pp. 360–370). Stroudsburg, PA: Association for Computational Linguistics.

Specia, L. (2011, May). Exploiting objective annotations for measuring translation post-editing effort. In *Proceedings of the 15th conference of the European Association for machine translation* (pp. 73–80). Switzerland: European Association for Machine Translation.

Specia, L., & Farzindar, A. (2010, November). Estimating machine translation post-editing effort with HTER. In *Proceedings of the second joint EM+/CNGL workshop bringing MT to the user: Research on integrating MT in the translation industry (JEC 10)* (pp. 33–41). Washington, DC: Association for Machine Translation in the Americas.

Štajner, S., & Hulpuş, I. (2018, August). Automatic assessment of conceptual text complexity using knowledge graphs. In *Proceedings of the 27th international conference on computational linguistics* (pp. 318–330). Stroudsburg, PA: Association for Computational Linguistics.

Tatsumi, M., & Roturier, J. (2010, November). Source text characteristics and technical and temporal post-editing effort: What is their relationship. In *Proceedings of the second joint EM+/CNGL workshop bringing MT to the user: Research on integrating MT in the translation industry (JEC 10)* (pp. 43–51). Washington, DC: Association for Machine Translation in the Americas.

Tu, Z., Lu, Z., Liu, Y., Liu, X., & Li, H. (2016). Modeling coverage for neural machine translation. In *Proceedings of the 54th Annual Meeting of the Association for Computational Linguistics* (Volume 1: Long Papers) (pp. 76–85). Berlin, Germany.

Vieira, L. N. (2014). Indices of cognitive effort in machine translation post-editing. *Machine Translation, 28*(3–4), 187–216. Berlin: Springer.

Vieira, L. N. (2017). From process to product: Links between post-editing effort and post-edited quality. In A. L. Jakobsen & B. Mesa-Lao (Eds.), *Translation in transition: Between cognition, computing and technology* (pp. 162–186). Amsterdam: John Benjamins. doi: 10.1075/btl.133.06vie

Vu, T., & Haffari, G. (2018). Automatic post-editing of machine translation: A neural programmer-interpreter approach. In *Proceedings of the 2018 conference on empirical methods in natural language processing* (pp. 3048–3053). Stroudsburg, PA: Association for Computational Linguistics.

5 Analyzing multiword term formation as a means to facilitate translation

Melania Cabezas-García

1 Introduction

Multiword terms (MWTs) are used both in general and specialized language texts. In specialized language, MWTs, such as *fixed-pitch wind turbine*, are especially frequent because of the multiple possibilities of conceptual combination that they provide. They reflect the conceptual systems in specialized domains and thus contribute to specialized knowledge transmission. Nevertheless, their analysis is extremely complex. Problematic aspects include their identification and structural disambiguation and semantic analysis as well as the specification of the relation between their constituents. All of these factors complicate their translation.

The semantic relations underlying MWTs and their bracketing or structural disambiguation have been the focus of considerable research. However, other issues that still need to be satisfactorily addressed include the analysis of highly specialized MWTs, their formation, and their composition in English as well as in other languages. More specifically, knowledge of MWT formation is essential for their translation and representation in terminographic resources.

This chapter presents a corpus-based analysis of MWT formation that provides further insights into the conceptual development of these terms and highlights the benefits of this information in translation. As part of this study, we compiled an English corpus of specialized texts on wind power (3,025,237 words). This research focused on English MWTs because English is the *lingua franca* of communication. The translation results are illustrated with Spanish examples.

English MWTs were extracted by means of corpus queries based on regular expressions. They were then semantically analyzed, which entailed the following: (i) bracketing; (ii) assignment of semantic categories; (iii) decoding the internal semantic relations by means of paraphrases; and (iv) semantic role labeling. This revealed the *microcontext* of each MWT, which explains their formation and productivity and facilitates their translation.

DOI: 10.4324/9781003102694-5

The rest of this paper is organized as follows. Section 2 discusses previous studies on MWT formation. Section 3 presents the materials and methods used in this research. Section 4 explains MWT formation by means of microcontexts and describes the usefulness of this analysis in translation. Finally, section 5 summarizes the conclusions that can be derived from this study.

2 Multiword term formation

Multiword terms (MWTs) are expressions in which the head is complemented by one or various modifiers. For example, in *floating offshore wind turbine*, the head, *turbine*, is modified by *floating*, *offshore*, and *wind*. MWTs are very frequent in English and Spanish (Nakov, 2013; Fernández Domínguez, 2019), and they are especially prominent in specialized discourse (Kageura, 2002; Faber, 2012; Nakov & Hearst, 2013; inter alia), thanks to their multiple possibilities of conceptual combination, which facilitate lexical and terminological expansion (Baldwin & Kim, 2010). MWTs thus contribute to specialized knowledge transmission.

MWTs have been a research focus in general linguistics, terminology, lexicography, computational linguistics, and psycholinguistics. Their identification in texts is often difficult since MWTs can be formed by various terms or even by general language words. Ascertaining structural dependencies can be very challenging in MWTs consisting of three or more elements. Semantic analysis can also be difficult, given the non-specification of the semantic relation between the constituents. Nor is their translation into other languages an easy task, either, because of the different patterns of term formation and the unsystematic treatment of MWTs in terminographic resources. In particular, the analysis of MWT formation facilitates translation.

To understand the generation and conceptualization of MWTs, it is necessary to first focus on their structural formation. Depending on their structure, they can be endocentric or exocentric (Levi, 1978; Nakov, 2013). In endocentric MWTs, one of the constituents is the head and the other is the modifier, which adds characteristics to the head. For example, in *offshore wind farm*, *offshore* modifies the head, *wind farm*. The binary structure in an endocentric MWT highlights its similarity to another concept since the head indicates the category to which the concept belongs, while the modifiers specify one or various distinguishing characteristics (Bowker, 1998; Gagné, 2000; Maguire et al., 2010). Therefore, the new concept resulting from the combination is usually a hyponym of the head (Downing, 1977; Sager, 1997; Cabezas-García & Faber, 2017). For example, *offshore wind farm* is a type of *wind farm*.

In contrast, exocentric MWTs are less frequent in general language and even less in specialized discourse. They lack a head (Levi, 1978; Nakov,

2013), as can be seen in *saber tooth*, in which neither constituent designates the category to which the MWT belongs (i.e., a feline). This explains their idiomatic and nontransparent nature. There is also a third group of coordinated MWTs in which both constituents are at the same level (e.g., *secretary-treasurer*) (Nakov, 2013; Fernández Domínguez, 2019). This paper focuses on endocentric MWTs since they are by far the most common MWTs in different languages and in specialized discourse.

The parts of speech and the place of MWT constituents are determined by the term formation patterns in the language in question (Levi, 1978; Sager, 1997; Fernández Domínguez, 2019). English MWTs are usually formed by premodification (Nakov, 2013). In other words, the head is located on the right, preceded by the modifiers, which can be nouns (*speed ratio*), adjectives (*reactive power*) or participles acting as adjectives (*rated power*). Unlike Germanic languages, such as English, noun stacking is not possible in Romance languages (Sager, 1997; Fernández Domínguez, 2019). Thus, MWTs in Romance languages, such as Spanish, are usually formed by postmodification in the form of adjectives (*potencia reactiva*) or prepositional phrases (*hueco de tensión*). Not surprisingly, these differences in structure can cause translation problems.

As for the underlying conceptualization influencing MWT formation, various studies point to the existence of concealed propositions, which include a predicate. Levi (1978) states that MWTs arise from either predicate deletion (e.g., virus *causes* disease > *viral disease*), or predicate nominalization (e.g., person that *analyzes* finance > *financial analyst*). Since the underlying propositions are conceptual, it is thus possible to tag predicate arguments with semantic roles (e.g., AGENT, PATIENT) and specify semantic relations (e.g., *affect*s, *causes*) that more accurately convey the conceptual formation of MWTs.

There are psycholinguistic theories that can explain the conceptual combination in MWTs. Murphy (1988) argues that the modifier fills one of the slots opened by the head. For example, in *apartment dog*, *apartment* fills the HABITAT slot of *dog*. Therefore, the meaning of the head determines the slots that can be opened as well as the modifiers that can fill those slots. Murphy's notion of slot opening is similar to that in Martin (1992) and Rosario et al. (2002) and is a basis for the *microcontexts* in this study (section 4). In contrast, Gagné (2000) proposes that MWTs are formed by means of a semantic relation between both concepts. For instance, a *snowman* is a man *made of* snow. However, as shall be seen, slots and semantic relations are not mutually exclusive.

In their study of semantic patterns in MWTs, Maguire et al. (2010) argue that semantically similar heads open slots that are filled by the same type of modifiers. In other words, the members of a semantic category usually combine in the same way (e.g., AREA+ANIMAL > ANIMAL *located_at* AREA [*water mammal, freshwater fish*]). Maguire et al. (2010) is key to our approach to MWT formation, since semantic categories can reveal regular patterns in MWTs, which can facilitate their translation.

Nevertheless, these theories of conceptual combination have been mostly applied to general language words. In terminology and specialized language, approaches to conceptual combination include the notion of *conceptual collocation* in Martin (1992), as applied in Heid (2001), L'Homme (2000), and conceptual frames in frame-based terminology (section 3) (Montero Martínez, 2008; Cabezas-García & Faber, 2018; Faber & Cabezas-García, 2019). Martin (1992) argues that specialized concepts have an argument structure that can be identified in their definition. These slots are filled with other concepts that have specific semantic characteristics. Therefore, he applies the idea of slot opening to specialized combinations, although these are not necessarily MWTs.

As a result, semantics guides the combination of concepts that generate MWTs. These concepts do not combine randomly and are subject to constraints. Entities usually combine with attributes (e.g., material, color, location, etc.), though not with causes or results, which would be typical of processes. For example, a flood has a result, but a table does not. These conceptual preferences are often reflected in recurrent patterns that we use to structure the world (Levi, 1978; Kageura, 2002; Rosario et al., 2002; Maguire et al., 2010). These patterns can be defined by means of semantic categories and roles.

For example, rather than saying that *cake* usually combines with *carrot* (*carrot cake*), it is more accurate to say that the conceptual category of FOOD usually co-occurs with the category of INGREDIENT. Since such categories are non-language-specific, this is true for both English (e.g., *meat pie, grilled chicken salad, mascarpone tart*) and Spanish (e.g., *empanada de atún, flan de huevo, pastel de berenjenas*). Levi (1978), Rosario et al. (2002) and Kageura (2002), among others, have analyzed MWT formation, based on recurrent combinations of categories. For instance, patterns such as PATIENT/VIRUS DISEASE (*influenza patient, AIDS survivor*) are common in the domain of biomedicine (Rosario et al., 2002).

Semantic roles can also be used to capture regularities in MWTs. This approach is less transparent than the previous one because of the frequent omission of the predicate (on which the semantic roles of the arguments depend). However, semantic roles reveal regularities, such as in *wind energy system* or *wind power plant*, both of which are composed of an INSTRUMENT (*system, plant*) and the PRODUCT of its action (*wind energy, wind power*).

These recurrent patterns of semantic categories and roles make it easier to infer the internal semantic relation in MWTs (Rosario et al., 2002; Maguire et al., 2010). For instance, Rosario et al. (2002, p. 3) determine that the categories BODY REGION and CARDIOVASCULAR SYSTEM co-occur in MWTs, such as *scalp artery*, *heel capillary* and *limb vein*, which encode the *located_at* relation. Therefore, it can be assumed that *pulmonary vein* also codifies this relation, because its constituents are similar. This approach can facilitate the understanding and translation of unknown MWTs, because as observed by Levi (1978), these frequent combinations will occur not only in English but probably also in other languages.

The combination of semantic categories and roles can be used to explain MWT formation. One of the few studies that integrates both approaches is Bouillon et al. (2012), who analyzed MWTs in French and Italian by tagging their constituents with categories (ARTIFACT, TIME PERIOD, etc.) and roles (AGENT, INSTRUMENT, etc.). An internal predicate is also specified. For example, in *freight train*, the underlying predicate is *transport*, which makes the semantic relation explicit.

Nevertheless, although semantic categories and roles are useful for the characterization of MWTs, the semantic relations are also necessary. These relations are often concealed (e.g., *offshore wind farm* > wind farm *located offshore*). Their specification is generally based on inventories of semantic relations (e.g., *cause*, *affect*, etc.) of differing granularity. For example, the PropBank inventory (Palmer et al., 2005) includes general relations, whereas there are also domain-specific taxonomies, such as Rosario et al. (2002) for the field of biomedicine.

Nevertheless, according to Jespersen (1942) and Downing (1977), the association between MWT constituents cannot be characterized by a closed inventory of relations. For this purpose, Lauer (1995) uses prepositional paraphrases (*olive oil* is *oil from olives*) and Nakov and Hearst (2006) use verbal paraphrases (*malaria mosquito* is a *mosquito that carries/spreads/transmits malaria*). In fact, verbal paraphrases (Nakov & Hearst, 2013; Nakov, 2013) are currently very popular among computational linguists, who use them to decode and characterize the internal semantic relation in MWTs.

Rather than an alternative to traditional taxonomies, paraphrases can be understood as a method to access relations. In other words, semantic relations and paraphrases are complementary approaches. The extraction of paraphrases can thus be used to represent the combination of concepts in an MWT, which can then be labeled with a semantic relation.

3 Materials and methods

Frame-based terminology (FBT) (Faber, 2012, 2015) is the theoretical framework applied in this study. FBT is a cognitive approach to terminology that focuses on the representation of specialized knowledge with a special focus on conceptual organization, the multidimensional nature of terminological units, and the extraction of semantic and syntactic information from multilingual corpora (Faber, 2009, p. 123). For the purposes of this study, we compiled an English corpus of specialized texts on wind power (3,025,237 words). The corpus analysis platform, Sketch Engine (www.sketchengine.eu/, Kilgarriff et al., 2014), was used to extract and analyze MWTs. MWTs were obtained by identifying five of the most relevant concepts in the wind power domain (i.e., *wind*, *turbine*, *power*, *generator*, and *voltage*). These terms were then queried by means of Corpus Query Language (CQL) expressions in order to elicit MWTs that contained these terms. Table 5.1 shows an example of a CQL query for MWT extraction:

Table 5.1 Example of CQL query to extract MWTs including a specific term (*generator*)

[tag="N.*|JJ.*|RB.*|VVN.*|VVG.*"]{1,}[lemma="generator"][tag!="N.*|JJ.*"]

The query in Table 5.1 searched for *generator* ([lemma="generator"]), which could be preceded by nouns, adjectives, adverbs, and past or present participles that appeared one or more times ([tag="N.*|JJ.*|RB.*|VVN.*| VVG.*"]{1,}). As reflected in the query, *generator* could not be followed by nouns or adjectives ([tag!="N.*|JJ.*"]) to prevent the resulting MWTs from being part of a longer sequence. It was thus possible to obtain MWTs such as *synchronous generator* or *doubly fed induction generator*.

By focusing on the 40 most frequent MWTs generated by each of the five key terms, we obtained a sample of 200 MWTs. After reviewing their concordances and discarding any erroneous or duplicated terms, the list was reduced to 182 MWTs. The analysis of these MWTS entailed: (i) bracketing, (ii) assigning semantic categories, (iii) decoding the internal semantic relation, and (iv) semantic role labeling.

To specify the semantic relation between MWT constituents, it was first necessary to ascertain the structure of MWTs with more than two elements because internal dependencies highlight the parts that are linked by the relation. MWT analysis must thus start with bracketing or structural disambiguation in order to reduce MWTs with more than two constituents (61 of the 182 MWTs) to their head and modifier. To do this, we used the protocol in Cabezas-García and León-Araúz (2019) to ascertain the structure of MWTs, as in [*wind turbine*] *rotor*. This protocol includes different corpus queries based on the linguistic properties of MWTs and recent advances in natural language processing that facilitate MWT bracketing. For example, *wind turbine rotor* was bracketed as [*wind turbine*] *rotor* because *wind turbine* was more frequent in the corpus than the other possible combination, *turbine rotor*. In addition to this type of search, the protocol includes other queries to solve bracketing.

Table 5.2 Assignment of semantic categories in *generator torque control*

generator torque control	
[generator torque]	ENTITY>FORCE>STRESS
control	PROCESS>CHANGE>CHANGE IN SIZE/INTENSITY

After determining their structure, the MWTs were assigned semantic categories. This inventory of categories had been developed in the LexiCon research group from the concepts included in EcoLexicon (https://ecolexicon.ugr.es/), a terminological knowledge base on the environment (San Martín et al., 2020), which is the practical application of FBT. The categories in this inventory are based on concept definitions and the contextual information in the EcoLexicon corpus. After determining the characteristics shared by concepts, the resulting inventory of semantic categories was hierarchically organized in five levels. The most general level consists of the starter ontological categories of ENTITY (mental and physical objects), PROCESS (events that last over a period of time), and ATTRIBUTE (characteristics of entities or processes). The other levels are more specific. These categories were assigned to the groups resulting from bracketing and were determined by consulting the definitions and contextual information in the wind energy corpus. Table 5.2 presents the annotation of *generator torque control*. Since the internal structure of this term was [*generator torque*] *control*, the modifier, *generator torque*, was assigned the ENTITY>FORCE>STRESS category, and the head, *control*, was assigned the PROCESS>CHANGE>CHANGE IN SIZE/INTENSITY category.

The internal semantic relation in MWTs was then analyzed. Verb paraphrases were first queried, and if no results were obtained, free paraphrases were searched for. The following CQL expression was queried to find verb paraphrases, which searched for the two main elements or groups in the MWT linked by a verb (Table 5.3):

Table 5.3 Example of a CQL query to extract verb paraphrases

([lemma="power"][]{0,10}[tag="V.*"][]{0,10}[lemma="curve"] within <s/>)| ([lemma="curve"][]{0,10}[tag="V.*"][]{0,10}[lemma="power"] within <s/>)

This expression, illustrated with *power curve*, searched for one of the elements of the MWT ([lemma="power"]) followed by a verb ([tag="V.*"]), which would represent the relation between the MWT constituents. This verb could be preceded or followed by 0 to 10 elements ([]{0,10}). The other MWT constituent was also searched for ([lemma="curve"]). Furthermore, paraphrases had to appear within the same sentence (within <s/>)

characteristics, including power curve the curve which plots the power output of a turbine as a function of the wind respectively. In Figures 3 and 4, the green curve represents practical output power ; the blue curve is for the prediction result of Wind turbine manufacturers provide power curves representing turbine power output as a function of wind speed (see Chapter

Figure 5.1 Sample of the verb paraphrases for *power curve*

since different sentences were not targeted. The symbol | was also included to indicate disjunction, and it was followed by the same expression in reverse order in order to find the constituents on either side of the verb. This expression obtained concordance lines such as those in Figure 5.1, in which *power* and *curve* are linked by verbs such as *plot* and *represent*, which indicate the conceptual proposition curve *represents* power.

However, verbs that clearly illustrate the internal relation in an MWT were not always found. In those cases, free paraphrases were used (i.e., occurrences of the MWT constituents in the corpus). They can be used to analyze the context in which these elements co-occur and thus to extract semantic features. For example, the following query was used to extract free paraphrases of *nominal voltage* (Table 5.4):

Table 5.4 Example of CQL query to extract free paraphrases

([lemma="nominal"][lemma!="voltage"][]{0,10}[lemma!="nominal"] [lemma="voltage"] within <s/>)| ([lemma!="nominal"][lemma="voltage"][]{0,10}[lemma="nominal"] [lemma!="voltage"] within <s/>)

The regular expression in Table 5.4 searches for one of the constituents of the MWT ([lemma="nominal"]), which could not be immediately followed by the other constituent ([lemma!="voltage"]) to avoid occurrences of the MWT itself. Then a span of 0 to 10 words was introduced ([]{0,10}), which was followed by the other MWT element ([lemma="voltage"]), which again could not be preceded by the previously included constituent ([lemma!="nominal"]). The query should appear in the same sentence (within <s/>). Finally, the disjunction symbol | was followed by the same sequence with the MWT constituents in reverse order. Free paraphrases referring to an element that was not present in the MWT (*value*) were obtained, which probably complicated the extraction of verb paraphrases:

1 It is essential that the *voltage is kept close to the nominal value*, in the entire power system.
2 The large-scale centralised power plants *keep the node voltages within the allowed deviation from their nominal value* and the number of dedicated voltage control devices is limited.
3 The voltage balance control scheme is reactivated and input capacitor *voltages quickly converge to nominal values*.

Analyzing multiword term formation 113

When MWT semantics could not be accessed by any of these means, the search for the MWT itself in the corpus was combined with the use of external terminological resources. Semantic relations were assigned from the head to the modifier since the directionality of relations can normally be alternated (*has_function* vs. *function_of*). The EcoLexicon inventory of relations was used (i.e., *type_of*, *part_of*, *made_of*, *delimited_by*, *located_at*, *takes_place_in*, *phase_of*, *affects*, *causes*, *attribute_of*, *opposite_of*, *studies*, *measures*, *represents*, *result_of*, *effected_by*, and *has_function*) in addition to the domain-specific *uses_resource*.

After identifying the conceptual propositions, semantic roles were assigned to the bracketing groups. Although semantic roles have been traditionally assigned to a predicate arguments, we labeled MWTs with semantic roles based on the conceptual propositions underlying these terms. These propositions included various concepts that were linked by a semantic relation. The assignment of semantic roles was thus based on the relation that linked the concepts and was not necessarily based on the explicit presence of a predicate (e.g., in *power station*, *station* is the AGENT that *causes* a PATIENT, *power*). An inventory of semantic roles developed in the LexiCon research group was used, which is inspired by the roles proposed in FrameNet (Fillmore, 1982), Role and Reference Grammar (Van Valin & LaPolla, 1997), and VerbNet (Kipper et al., 2004). The roles included were AGENT, THEME, POSSESSOR, PATIENT, INSTRUMENT, LOCATION, and DESCRIPTIVE. For example, *wind park* was annotated as *wind*[INSTRUMENT] *park*[AGENT] because the conceptual proposition was park *uses_resource* wind. In conclusion, this analysis provided valuable insights into MWT formation.

4 Microcontexts in the formation and translation of multiword terms

Corpus analysis made it possible to investigate MWT formation from a conceptual perspective and provided information that was useful for MWT translation. First, by exploring how semantic categories combined within MWTs, recurrent patterns were found that are directly related to the microcontexts explained in this section. For instance, the combination of the ATTRIBUTE and ENTITY>CREATION categories produced 32 MWTs, such as *asynchronous generator* and *commercial wind turbine*. Also discovered were term variants (e.g., synonyms of *wind farm* such as *wind plant*, *wind power station*, etc.) and conceptual variants (e.g., *wind power* as an attribute of wind or the electricity resulting from its use).

In regard to translation, term variation should be acknowledged in the source language since this facilitates the identification of variants in the target language. Furthermore, the preference for one variant or another (both in the source and target languages) as well as possible cognitive or stylistic implications should also be considered. Along these lines, when translating term variants, which are often MWTs (León-Araúz et al., 2020; León-Araúz & Cabezas-García, 2020), translators or terminologists must consider whether this variation should be respected (because it performs cognitive or communicative functions [Fernández Silva & Kerremans, 2011]) or if it should be avoided for the sake of consistency.

Conceptual variation also has repercussions on translation. It may hinder the understanding of an MWT and thus of a term's combinatorial potential. For example, when *power* is understood as an attribute, it combines with verbs such as *extract* or *absorb*. In contrast, when *power* is understood as electricity, it tends to co-occur with predicates such as *store* or *consume*. However, this meaning coincidence in the same term is not necessarily reproduced in other languages. In Spanish, *power* is usually translated as *energía* or *electricidad* when it means electrical energy. In contrast, its usual equivalent when it refers to an attribute is *potencia*. Derived MWTs also follow this pattern. Therefore, automatically calquing the term in the target language can be dangerous since it can lead to the use of equivalents that do not convey the same meaning.

Another type of conceptual variation is related to multidimensionality or the description of the same concept from different perspectives. This often gives rise to term variants resulting from different conceptualizations. Multidimensionality can affect MWT form since the dimension that is most emphasized in the immediate context is the one that appears in first position in the MWT (Bowker, 1998, p. 490). For example, in a color-related context, *color flatbed scanner* will be preferred over *flatbed color scanner* because *color* is named first. This is also the case in the Spanish variants, for example *densidad espectral de potencia* and *densidad de potencia espectral*, in which the term closer to the head is cognitively prominent. However, their English correspondences (*power spectrum* and *power spectral density*) do not permit this formal variation, which highlights the differences between the source and target languages.

Semantic relations also have a central role in microcontexts. The use of paraphrases to find this relation proved to be helpful in translation. First, verb paraphrases retrieved verbs that further characterize the relation between the MWT constituents, which clarified their meaning (e.g., verbs such as *control, adjust, fluctuate*, or *vary* specify the *affects* relation). Second, verb paraphrases can be used to obtain additional semantic and contextual information, which is also helpful. This can be observed in the following paraphrase for *wind penetration*, which reveals the place where wind energy *penetrates* or is integrated: "Wind has already made solid steps forward, penetrating national transmission systems by as much as 10 per cent in several markets and as much as 21 per cent in Denmark".

Paraphrases also uncovered elements that were not explicit in MWTs. For example, paraphrases of *floating turbine* showed that the turbine *is installed on a floating foundation/is set on a floating column/is installed on a floating platform*. Therefore, the turbine floats because it is located on supporting elements such as bases, columns or platforms. These elements are not explicitly mentioned in the MWT. Free paraphrases also revealed additional arguments, concealed constituents of the MWT, and variants.

Once the internal semantic relation was identified, the semantic roles of the MWT constituents in the underlying conceptual proposition were analyzed. This made it possible to capture regularities. For example, the POSSESSOR-THEME role scheme generated 56 MWTs, such as *line-to-neutral voltage* or *wind turbine blade*. Such constraints are a key factor in *microcontexts*.

To analyze MWT formation in the wind power domain, the basic premise was that semantically similar units open slots that are filled by other units that also share conceptual features. This produces specialized combinations. These slots are a kind of argument structure and can be perceived in a concept definition.

Semantically similar units were grouped together (i.e., MWTs whose heads belonged to the same semantic category). The semantic categories of these heads were regarded as *nuclear categories*. For example, *turbine*, *converter*, *grid*, *plant*, or *farm*, among other terms, refer to specific concepts of the nuclear category ENTITY>CREATION. To explore whether these different terms had the same combination patterns, we compared the semantic categories and roles with which they co-occurred as well as the relations that they encoded.

The analysis of the combinatorial potential of nuclear categories showed that the concepts or terms belonging to a certain nuclear category have similar co-occurrence patterns. This similarity in the combinations of MWTs led to the specification of *microcontexts*, which account for the productivity in MWT formation. Microcontexts are a kind of argument structure of the MWT head. In other words, nuclear semantic categories open one or several slots based on their meaning. These slots determine the MWTs that can be formed to specify that nuclear category. The analysis of MWT formation through their microcontexts facilitates the understanding of these units and their translation.

This process is illustrated with the category of ENTITY>CREATION, which was particularly productive. Table 5.5 shows the slots opened by the ENTITY>CREATION category. The left column specifies the different slots that were labeled with their role in the MWT conceptual proposition. The semantic categories that can fill these slots are shown, as well as the semantic relation encoded. Finally, the rightmost column includes a sample of the MWTs that exhibit that combination pattern.

116 Melania Cabezas-García

Table 5.5 Slots opened by the ENTITY>CREATION category

ENTITY>CREATION

Slot (role)	Category	Relation	Examples
PATIENT	PROCESS>MOVEMENT>ENERGY MOVEMENT	causes affects	AC generator voltage source converter
INSTRUMENT	ENTITY>MATTER ENTITY>FORCE PROCESS>MOVEMENT	uses_resource	steam generator wind farm
DESCRIPTIVE	ATTRIBUTE ENTITY>CREATION>ARTIFACT> INSTRUMENT>TRANSFORMING INSTRUMENT	has_attribute has_function has_type	vertical axis wind turbine large wind farm
LOCATION	ATTRIBUTE>LOCATION	located_at	offshore wind turbine onshore wind farm
POSSESSOR	ENTITY>CREATION>ARTIFACT> INSTRUMENT>TRANSFORMING INSTRUMENT	part_of	generator rotor wind turbine generator
THEME (PART)	ENTITY>MATTER>SOLID MATTER>MATERIAL ENTITY>CREATION>ARTIFACT> INSTRUMENT>TRANSFORMING INSTRUMENT	has_part	permanent magnet generator wound rotor induction generator

The ENTITY>CREATION category opens the following slots: PATIENT, INSTRUMENT, DESCRIPTIVE, LOCATION, POSSESSOR, and THEME (PART). The PATIENT slot alludes to the concept that suffers the action carried out by the head. This slot was always filled by the PROCESS>MOVEMENT>ENERGY MOVEMENT category, as shown in *AC generator* and *voltage source converter*. However, the PATIENT can have two different conceptualizations, depending on the relation encoded with the head.

On the one hand, the PATIENT can be a concept that is converted or transported when this is the action carried out by the ENTITY>CREATION category. The internal relation is thus *affects* (converter *affects* voltage source). This pattern occurred in MWTs generated by the heads *converter, inverter*, and *grid* in this study.

On the other hand, the ENTITY>CREATION category can also emphasize the production phase. In those cases, the PATIENT is understood as the concept resulting from this production and the relation encoded is *causes*. This was a frequent pattern in MWTs whose head is *generator, plant* or *station* (generator *causes* AC). As can be observed, the category of ENTITY>CREATION is specified by indicating the PATIENT or concept that suffers the action.

The INSTRUMENT slot further specified the concept employed by ENTITY>CREATION to perform the activity. Two types of concept usually fill this slot: (i) concepts referring to the external resource used (e.g., *steam generator*, *wind farm*), which belong to ENTITY>MATTER or PROCESS>MOVEMENT; (ii) concepts referring to the force or materials used to generate motion (e.g., *induction generator*, *impulse turbine*), which belong to ENTITY>FORCE and ENTITY>MATTER. The resources used are obviously quite diverse since they can be fluids, chemicals, gases, etc. (ENTITY>MATTER) as well as processes such as wind or induction. Evidently, the characteristics of the concepts in ENTITY>CREATION (*generator, turbine, farm*, etc.) depend on the resource used. The relation codified was always *uses_resource*. This slot was opened by the different concepts belonging to ENTITY>CREATION, except for the head *grid*, which focuses on the transported concept (*power grid*) rather than on the instrument employed for transport.

The DESCRIPTIVE slot was filled by features that describe ENTITY>CREATION. Since these are considered to be ATTRIBUTES (e.g., physical attributes, magnitudes), the internal semantic relation is *has_attribute* (e.g., in *vertical axis wind turbine*, wind turbine *has_attribute* vertical axis). However, there are two exceptions that encode another relation. First, in *commercial wind turbine*, the *has_function* relation is activated since the concept is a wind turbine for commercial use. However, *commercial* is still a descriptive feature of the head, which is why it has the DESCRIPTIVE role. Second, *wind turbine generator* encodes the *has_type* relation since a wind turbine is a type of generating instrument. In this case, the semantic category filling the slot is not ATTRIBUTE, but rather ENTITY>CREATION>ARTIFACT>INSTRUMENT> TRANSFORMING INSTRUMENT. Nevertheless, *wind turbine* still has a DESCRIPTIVE role. In conclusion, even though these two concepts are not attributes, they allude to functions and subtypes, which are also descriptive features.

The LOCATION slot was also opened, which refers to the place where ENTITY>CREATION is situated. It was filled with the ATTRIBUTE>LOCATION category, and the relation is *located_at* (e.g., in *offshore wind turbine*, wind turbine *located* offshore).

Furthermore, the POSSESSOR slot indicates the more general category to which the nuclear category belongs. In our sample, this slot was opened by transforming instruments, such as *generator* or *turbine*. It was filled by concepts of the same category, so that two similar concepts (transforming instruments) combined to form an MWT. The relation is *part_of* (e.g., in *generator rotor*, rotor *part_of* generator). Therefore, the MWTs that fill this slot usually designate the parts of a transforming instrument that are responsible for transformation (e.g., *rotor generator*, *wind turbine generator*).

Finally, the nuclear category of ENTITY>CREATION also opened the THEME (PART) slot, which is activated when ENTITY>CREATION is understood as a POSSESSOR. Therefore, this slot indicates its parts as well as its characteristics. Only transforming instruments opened this slot in our sample, which is filled by the semantic category of ENTITY>MATTER>SOLID MATTER>MATERIAL. This is in the case of the materials of the ENTITY, such as *permanent magnet* in *permanent magnet generator*. It also applies to ENTITY>CREATION>ARTIFACT> INSTRUMENT> TRANSFORMING INSTRUMENT as reflected in the transforming components of the ENTITY (e.g., *wound rotor* in *wound rotor induction generator*). In all cases, the internal relation is *has_part*.

The analysis of the slots opened by ENTITY>CREATION revealed the high productivity of this category for producing MWTs (67 MWTs followed these combination patterns). Furthermore, several of these slots were opened by the different concepts included in the category of ENTITY>CREATION (e.g., *generator*, *grid*, *farm*), which highlights the similarity of their combination patterns. These slots were PATIENT, INSTRUMENT, DESCRIPTIVE, and LOCATION, which were found to be present in almost all the concepts. These slots thus form the *argument structure* or microcontext of the nuclear category of ENTITY>CREATION.

In conclusion, microcontexts are a new approach to the classic slot-filling procedure, which reflect the conceptual mechanism that generates MWTs in specialized discourse. They can be understood as semantic profiles of the category in question and can be helpful during the translation process.

When translating, they can be used to access and recreate the conceptual map of the specialized domain. Since the analysis of microcontexts entails an exploration of the conceptual propositions underlying MWTs, this provides a view of the conceptual system, which is non-language-specific and thus essential in translation. For example, the analysis of the slots opened by *turbine* discloses relations that are encoded with other concepts: (i) *uses_resource* (activated in MWTs such as *gas turbine*, *hydraulic turbine*, and *wind turbine*); (ii) *has_attribute* (activated in *fixed-speed wind turbine* and *downwind turbine*); (iii) *located_at* (activated in *onshore turbine* and *offshore turbine*); and (iv) *has_part* (activated in *rotor turbine* and *wind turbine generator*). Knowledge of related concepts and thus of the specialized domain is a necessity when rendering a text into another language.

Additionally, microcontexts and definitions are interrelated because microcontexts can be inferred from the definitions of concepts. Furthermore, the analysis of the MWTs generated from a head can be used to delimit the defining features of this nuclear concept. For instance, some of the MWTs formed from *plant* in the field of electrical energy include *power plant*, *wind power plant*, *wind plant*, *hydropower plant*, or *thermal power plant*. In these MWTs, the head (*plant*) belongs to the category of

ENTITY>CREATION>STRUCTURE and opens the PATIENT (*power*) and INSTRUMENT (*wind, hydro-, thermal*) slots. Therefore, based on this information, *plant* can be defined as follows:
  plant structure that converts some form of energy into electrical energy.

Concept clarification in the form of a definition is helpful in translation since it provides translators with the conceptual characteristics from which the equivalent will emerge and can be used to verify conceptual correspondence.

Furthermore, MWTs can be formed by filling one or several slots. This often occurs in MWTs with three or more constituents. For example, in *wound rotor induction generator*, *generator*, which is the head, first activates the INSTRUMENT slot (*induction*) and then the THEME (PART) slot (*wound rotor*). Since this type of MWT is longer and cognitively more complex, it can be the source of translation problems. For this reason, the conceptual analysis of microcontexts can be used to decode and clarify this type of terms.

Analyzing microcontexts and thus the regular combination patterns that often occur in MWTs facilitates the inference of new MWTs by comparing them with already known patterns. For example, if *voltage source converter* fills the PATIENT slot with the category of PROCESS>MOVEMENT>ENERGY MOVEMENT and encodes the *affects* relation, the same pattern probably occurs in *voltage source inverter*. This is also true of interlinguistic correspondences, such as *convertidor en fuente de tensión* [*voltage source converter*] or *inversor en fuente de tensión* [*voltage source inverter*], which can also be easily inferred by comparison with existing patterns. This shortens the time devoted to understanding the concept, which in turn also shortens the translation process.

In addition, knowledge of the slots opened by an MWT head in a source language simplifies the identification of the different combinations of this head in the target language. MWTs are rarely translated word for word. For this reason, the different slots that can be opened should be identified since the slots filled by the equivalents can differ from those in the source language.

For example, Termium Plus (www.btb.termiumplus.gc.ca/) includes the following definition for *generating station*: "unit that converts some form of energy into electrical energy". The English term (*generating station*) refers to energy generation, whereas its equivalent in Spanish (*central eléctrica*) specifies the resulting electricity. As can be observed, a slot can be omitted in one language and made explicit in another. For instance, *aerogenerador* refers specifically to the generation activity, which does not occur in its equivalent, *wind turbine*. Accordingly, the same slot can be reproduced in both languages by means of different semantic categories or roles (*rated power, rated output > potencia nominal, potencia nominal de salida*). Therefore, a good command of microcontexts provides access to the possible combinations in the source and target languages and accelerates the search process.

To conclude, microcontexts provide valuable insights regarding the conceptual generation of MWTs. For this reason, a better understanding of their formation facilitates and simplifies the identification of translation equivalents.

5 Conclusions

This chapter has described a corpus-based study of the conceptual formation of MWTs. The notion of *microcontexts* is based on research on multiword expressions in disciplines such as general linguistics, terminology, computational linguistics, and psycholinguistics. Equivalent terms are generally formed by a different number and type of elements. In the case of MWTs, word-for-word translations are rare (e.g., *freno aerodinámico* > *flap*). That is why the translation of MWTs should be based on conceptual and contextual analysis. The analysis of MWT formation by means of microcontexts provides translators with the necessary conceptual tools before establishing equivalences.

Consequently, microcontexts can be used to access the underlying conceptual system, craft definitions, clarify complex terms, and infer new MWTs both in the source and target language. Furthermore, the semantic analysis of conceptual categories, relations, and roles is also useful for translation. In particular, the presence of term and concept variation was highlighted, which has important repercussions for translation, as well as the usefulness of paraphrases for the extraction of conceptual and contextual information. In conclusion, this research provided a new perspective on MWT analysis that focuses on conceptual analysis, which is the basis of translation.

Acknowledgments

This research was carried out as part of project FFI2017–89127-P, Translation-Oriented Terminology Tools for Environmental Texts (TOTEM), funded by the Spanish Ministry of Economy and Competitiveness.

References

Baldwin, T., & Kim, S. N. (2010). Multiword expressions. In N. Indurkhya & F. J. Damerau (Eds.), *Handbook of natural language processing* (2nd ed., pp. 267–292). Boca Ratón: CRC Press.

Bouillon, P., Jezek, E., Melloni, C., & Picton, A. (2012). Annotating qualia relations in Italian and French complex nominals. In N. Calzolari, et al. (Eds.), *Proceedings of the 8th international conference on language resources and evaluation (LREC 2012)* (pp. 1527–1532). Istanbul: ELRA.

Bowker, L. (1998). Using specialized monolingual native-language corpora as a translation resource: A pilot study. *Meta, 43*(4), 631–651.
Cabezas García, M., & Faber, P. (2017). A semantic approach to the inclusion of complex nominals in English terminographic resources. In R. Mitkov (Ed.), *Computational and corpus-based phraseology* (pp. 145–159). Lecture Notes in Computer Science 10596. Cham: Springer.
Cabezas García, M., & Faber, P. (2018). Phraseology in specialized resources: An approach to complex nominals. *Lexicography, 5*(1), 55–83.
Cabezas García, M., & León Araúz, P. (2019). On the structural disambiguation of multi-word terms. In G. Corpas Pastor & R. Mitkov (Eds.), *Computational and corpus-based phraseology* (pp. 46–60). Lecture Notes in Computer Science, 11755. Cham: Springer.
Downing, P. (1977). On the creation and use of English compound nouns. *Language, 53*, 810–842.
Faber, P. (2009). The cognitive shift in terminology and specialized translation. *MonTI. Monografías de Traducción e Interpretación, 1*, 107–134.
Faber, P. (2012). *A cognitive linguistics view of terminology and specialized language*. Berlin, Boston: De Gruyter Mouton.
Faber, P. (2015). Frames as a framework for terminology. In H. J. Kockaert & F. Steurs (Eds.), *Handbook of terminology* (Vol. 1, pp. 14–33). Amsterdam, Philadelphia: John Benjamins.
Faber, P., & Cabezas García, M. (2019). Specialized knowledge representation: From terms to frames. *Research in Language, 17*(2), 197–211.
Fernández Domínguez, J. (2019). Compounds and multi-word expressions in Spanish. In B. Schlücker (Ed.), *Complex lexical units: Compounds and multi-word expressions* (pp. 189–219). Berlin, Boston: De Gruyter.
Fernández Silva, S., & Kerremans, K. (2011). Terminological variation in source texts and translations: A pilot study. *Meta. Journal des Traducteurs, 56*(2), 318–335.
Fillmore, C. J. (1982). Frame semantics. In The Linguistic Society of Korea (Ed.), *Linguistics in the morning calm* (pp. 111–137). Seoul: Hanshin.
Gagné, C. L. (2000). Relational-based combinations versus property-based combinations: A test of the CARIN theory and the dual-process theory of conceptual combination. *Journal of Memory and Language, 42*, 365–389.
Heid, U. (2001). Collocations in sublanguage texts: Extraction from corpora. In S. E. Wright & G. Budin (Eds.), *Handbook of terminology management. Volume 2: Applications-oriented terminology management* (pp. 788–808). Amsterdam, Philadelphia: John Benjamins.
Jespersen, O. (1942). *A modern English grammar: On historical principles*. Copenhagen: Munksgaard.
Kageura, K. (2002). *The dynamics of terminology: A descriptive theory of term formation and terminological growth*. Amsterdam: John Benjamins.
Kilgarriff, A., Baisa, V., Bušta, J., Jakubíček, M., Kovář, V., Michelfeit, J., Rychlý, P., & Suchomel, V. (2014). The sketch engine: Ten years on. *Lexicography, 1*(1), 7–36.
Kipper, K., Snyder, B., & Palmer, M. (2004). Extending a verb-lexicon using a semantically annotated corpus. In *Proceedings of the 4th international conference on language resources and evaluation (LREC 2004)* (pp. 1557–1560). Lisbon: ELRA.

Lauer, M. (1995). *Designing statistical language learners: Experiments on noun compounds* (PhD thesis). Macquarie University, Sydney.

León-Araúz, P., & Cabezas-García, M. (2020). Term and translation variation of multiword terms. *MonTI. Monografías de Traducción e Interpretación*. Special Issue 6, 210–247.

León-Araúz, P., Cabezas-García, M., & Reimerink, A. (2020). Representing multiword term variation in a terminological knowledge base: A corpus-based study. In *Proceedings of the 12th conference on language resources and evaluation (LREC 2020)* (pp. 2351–2360). Marseille: ELRA.

Levi, J. (1978). *The syntax and semantics of complex nominals*. New York: Academic Press.

L'Homme, M. C. (2000). Understanding specialized lexical combinations. *Terminology*, 6(1), 89–110.

Maguire, P., Wisniewski, E. J., & Storms, G. (2010). A corpus study of semantic patterns in compounding. *Corpus Linguistics and Linguistic Theory*, 6(1), 49–73.

Martin, W. (1992). Remarks on collocations in sublanguages. *Terminologie et Traduction*, 2(3), 157–164.

Montero Martínez, S. (2008). A constructional approach to terminological phrasemes. In E. Bernal & J. DeCesaris (Eds.), *Proceedings of the XIII EURALEX international congress* (pp. 1015–1022). Barcelona: Institut Universitari de Lingüística Aplicada/Documenta Universitaria.

Murphy, G. L. (1988). Comprehending complex concepts. *Cognitive Science*, 12, 529–562.

Nakov, P. (2013). On the interpretation of noun compounds: Syntax, semantics, and entailment. *Natural Language Engineering*, 19, 291–330.

Nakov, P., & Hearst, M. (2006). Using verbs to characterize noun-noun relations. In J. Euzenat & J. Domingue (Eds.), *Artificial intelligence: Methodology, systems, and applications: AIMSA 2006* (pp. 233–244). Berlin: Springer.

Nakov, P., & Hearst, M. (2013). Semantic interpretation of noun compounds using verbal and other paraphrases. *ACM Transactions on Speech and Language Processing*, 10(3), 1–51.

Palmer, M., Gildea, D., & Kingsbury, P. (2005). The proposition bank: An annotated corpus of semantic roles. *Computational Linguistics*, 31(1), 71–106.

Rosario, B., Hearst, M., & Fillmore, C. J. (2002). The descent of hierarchy, and selection in relational semantics. In P. Isabelle (Ed.), *Proceedings of the 40th annual meeting of the association for computational linguistics* (pp. 247–254). Philadelphia: ACL.

Sager, J. C. (1997). Term formation. In S. E. Wright & G. Budin (Eds.), *Handbook of terminology management. Volume 1: Basic aspects of terminology management* (pp. 25–41). Amsterdam, Philadelphia: John Benjamins.

San Martín, A., Cabezas-García, M., Buendía-Castro, M., Sánchez-Cárdenas, B., León-Araúz, P., Reimerink, A., & Faber, P. (2020). Presente y futuro de la base de conocimiento terminológica EcoLexicon. *Onomázein*, 49, 174–202.

Van Valin, R. D., & LaPolla, R. J. (1997). *Syntax: Structure, meaning, and function*. Cambridge: Cambridge University Press.

Index

Page numbers in *italics* indicate figures and page numbers in **bold** indicate tables.

Allan, K. 5–6, 10–13
Animal Farm (Orwell): cohesion words 72–73; corpus methods for xiv, 60–65, 67–68, 70–77; descriptive statistics 67–68; distance measures 68, **69**, 70, *70*, 71; human translations 64–65, 67–68, 73–74, 77; keyword analysis 71–72, **72**, 73–77; machine translations 63–64, **64**, 67, 73, 77; MDS analysis 68, 70, 72, 77; research data 61–63; Russian translations of 58, 60–65, **66**, 67–68, 70–77; STTR index 68; visual impressions 63–64
Askari, F. 8
Ayonrinde, O. 3
Azari, R. 9

BabelDr machine translation system: doctor input 2, 8–9; medical communication and xiii, 2; nonmedical translations 9; Persian translations 2, 8–9, **9**, 10, 18–19; sexual health questions 2
Baker, M. 26, 48
Bakhtiar, M. 5, 7–8, 12
Berber-Sardinha, T. 30, 32
Berman, Antoine 57
Bespalova, L. G. 61, 63, 65, **66**, 67, 70, 72–74, 76
Biber, D.: dimension concepts xiii, 31, 35, 37–38, *39*, 40–42, *43*, 47–48, *49*, 50–52; linguistic features and 30, 36; MDA and xiii, 27–35; on prepared and spontaneous speeches 41–42, 47; on "the scene" 33; on "the situation" 33–34; THAT and 48
Bible 58, 78
Bouillon, P. xiii, 109
Brezina, V. xiii, 30, 35, 37
Brookey, J. 14
Brown, E. 3, 15
Brown, P. 33
Burridge, K. 5–6, 10–11, 13
Bussmann, H. 4

Cabezas-García, M. xiv, 110
Calzada Pérez, M. xiii
Carroll, J. 28
Casas Gómez, M. 5
CD *see* Congreso de los Diputados (CD)
Chafe, W. 28
Cheesman, T. 57, 78
cohesion words 72–74
communication strategies (CSs): deletion and **11**, 13, 16; doctors and 3; euphemisms and 3–7, 10–11, **11**, 12, 15, **16**, 19; implication and 12–13; metonymy and 15, 17; nonmedical translations 16, **16**, 17; paraphrasing 10, **11**, 14–15, 17; Persian health communication 3, 7–11, **11**, 12–16, **16**, 17, 19; sexual health questions and 2, 16–17; transliteration and 10–11, **11**, 12, 16; using formal words 10, **11**, 13–14, **16**
conceptual collocation 108

124 Index

conceptual text complexity: post-editing quality and 83–84, 96–97, **98**, 100–101; semantic annotations and 83–84, 87, 93–94; semantic relations and 83, 100–101
conceptual variation 113–115
Conference on Machine Translation (WMT19) 83
Congreso de los Diputados (CD) 34
contextualization cues 4
corpus-based translation studies (CTS): Bible and 58, 78; development of 26; distance measures 58–59; English–Brazilian Portuguese post-editing 86, 91–92, 101; interdisciplinary 27; keyword analysis 59–60; limitations in 26–27; multifactorial 27; multimethodological 27; multiword terms (MWTs) and 105, 109–110, 113, 120; retranslations and 57–65, 67–68, 70–78
Corpus Query Language (CQL) 110, **110**, **111**
Costa, F. A. xiv, 86
CQL *see* Corpus Query Language (CQL)
cultural differences 2–4, 19

DeepL Translator 88, 95
definitions 118–119
Delaere, I. 32–33, 48, 50
deletion 11, **11**, 13, 16
De Sutter, G. xiii, 26–28, 32–33, 48, 50–51
distance measures 58–59, 68, **69**, 70, *70*, 71
Downing, P. 109

EcoLexicon 111–112
ECPC parliamentary discourse: dimension 1 analysis 37–40, *40*, 41–42; dimension 2 analysis 42, 44, *44*, 45–47; dimension 6 analysis 47–48, 50, *50*, 51; EP speeches 45; interventions in 45–46; LSTO results *36*; MDA and 27–28, 34–37, 47, 51; methodology of 34–37; narrative concerns in 45–47; text editing in 40–41; THAT in 48, 50–51; translated/non-translated Englishes in 28, 45–47; *see also* European Parliament (EP) speeches; House of Commons (HC) speeches
empirical translation studies (ETS) xiii, 28
English: euphemisms and 12; as *lingua franca* 105; multiword terms (MWTs) and 105–107; particles in 73; translated/non-translated 27–28, 47
English–Brazilian Portuguese translations: corpus methods for 86, 92, 101; human post-editing of 88–90; machine translations 88; post-editing quality and 84–86, 95–96, 101
EP *see* European Parliament (EP)
Ervin-Tripp, S. 28
euphemisms: as communication strategy 2–7, 10, **11**, 15, **16**, 19; defining 5–6; deletion and 11, **11**, 13, 16; implication and 12–13; medical communication and 2–3, 6–7; Persian medical communication and 7–9, **9**, **11**, 12, 17–18; sexual health questions and 2, 7, 10–13, 17; taboo language and 4–5, 7; taboo-related diseases and 7–8, 10–11; transliteration and 10–11, **11**, 12; types of 10–11, **11**
European Comparable and Parallel Corpus Archive of European Parliamentary Discourse (ECPC) 27, 34, 51; *see also* ECPC parliamentary discourse
European Parliament (EP) speeches: interventions in 45–46; narrative concerns in 45–47; text editing in 40–41; THAT in 50; time constraints in 44–45; translated/non-translated Englishes in 28, 35, 40–41, 45–47; *see also* ECPC parliamentary discourse

Farrington, C. 15
Ferreira, T. C. xiv
Fillmore, C. J. xiv
Finegan, E. 28
Firth, J. R. 28
Flanagan, K. 57

formal word use 10, **11**, 13–14, 16, **16**, 17–18
frame-based terminology (FBT) 109–111
FrameNet xiv, 113
Fraser, C. 33
frequency lists comparison 58–59
Friginal, E. 31, 35

Gagné, C. L. 107
García Márquez, G. 57
Goethe, J. W. von 57
Google Translate 2
Graham, S. 14

Halimi, S. A. xiii
Halliday, M. 28
Hardy, J. A. 31, 35
HC *see* House of Commons (HC)
Hearst, M. 109
Heid, U. 108
Hendrickson, M. A. 14
House of Commons (HC) speeches: interventions in 46; text editing in 40–41; THAT in 50; time constraints in 41; translated/non-translated Englishes in 28, 34–35; *see also* ECPC parliamentary discourse
Hu, X. 32
Hulpuş, I. 83
human translations: *Animal Farm* (Orwell) and 60–61, 64–65, 67–68, 72–74, 77; cohesion words 72–73; computer-aided 83, 85; length of 67; STTR index 68
Hymes, D. 28, 33

implication 12–13

Jespersen, O. 109
Ji, M. 32
Jones, H. 58

Kageura, K. 108
keyword analysis: cohesion words 72–74; corpus-based translation and 59–60; keyword lists 71–72, **72**; nouns and verbs 74–77; speech statistics in **73**
Kibirskij, S. 61, 63, 65, **66**, 73–74
Kilgarriff, A. xiv, 59

Kriger, M. 61, 63–65, **66**, 71–72, **72**, 73–74, 76
Kruger, H. 32–33

Lancaster Stats Tool Online (LSTO) xiii, 37
language barriers 1–3
Latifnejad Roudsari, R. 8
Lauer, M. 109
Lefer, M. A. xiii, 26–28, 32–33, 50–51
Lefevere, A. 33
León Araúz, P. 110
Levi, J. 107–109
LexiCon research group 111, 113
lexicons 58
LF Aligner 61
L'Homme, M. C. 108
Longacre, R. 28
LSTO *see* Lancaster Stats Tool Online (LSTO)

machine translations: *Animal Farm* (Orwell) and 60–61, 63–64, **64**, 67, 73, 77; English–Brazilian Portuguese 88; human post-editing of 83–85, 88–90, 97, 99, **99**; improvement in 83; quality and 94, 99, **99**; semantic annotations and xiv, 92; text cohesion and 72; *see also* phraselators
Maguire, P. 107–108
Martin, J. R. 34
Martin, W. 107–108
MAT xiii, 36–37
MDA *see* multidimensional analysis (MDA)
MDS *see* multidimensional scaling (MDS)
medical communication: contextualization cues xiii, 4; cultural differences and 3–4, 6, 19; emergency health care and 1–3; euphemisms and 2–4, 6–7; language barriers and 1–3; taboo words and 4; *see also* communication strategies (CSs); Persian health communication; sexual health communication
medical practice 3–4, 6
Meira, W., Jr. xiv
metonymy 15, 17

126 *Index*

microcontexts 105, 113–120
Microsoft Translator 58, 61, **66**
Mikhailov, M. xiv
MirzaiiNajmabadi, K. 8
Mosavi, S. A. 8
multidimensional analysis (MDA): Biber on 28–34; conceptual variation and 114; development of 28–29, 32; dimensions and 31, 37–42, 44–48, 50–52; empirical translation studies and xiii; features and assumptions of 29; interdisciplinary 27, 29; linguistic features and 30, 36; parliamentary discourse and 27–28, 34–37, 47, 51; scene in 33–34; situation in 33–34; stages of 29–32; technical-inspirational/imaginative requirements of 32; translation studies and 27–28, 32–34, 51–52
multidimensional scaling (MDS) xiv, 68, 70, 72
multivariate statistics 29–30, 32–33
multiword terms (MWTs): analysis of xiv, 105–106, 110, 113, 115, 118–120; concept definitions and 118–119; conceptual collocation in 108; conceptual combinations in 107–108; conceptual variation in 113–115; corpus methods for 105, 109–110, 113, 120; CQL query 110, **110, 111**; endocentric 106–107; exocentric 106–107; formation patterns 107; free paraphrases 111–112, **112**; microcontexts in 105, 113–120; multidimensionality and 114–115; predicate deletions/nominalizations 107; semantic categories and 105–111, **112**, 113, 115–116, **116**, 117–118; semantic patterns in 107–108; semantic relations and 109–115, 117; semantic roles and 105, 107–110, 113; specialized knowledge transmission and 105–106; structural formation of 106–107; term variants 113–114; verb paraphrases 109, 111, **111**, 112, *112*, 114–115
Munday, J. 34, 57
Murphy, G. L. 107
MWT *see* multiword terms (MWTs)

Nakov, P. 109
neural machine translation (NMT) 88
Nida, E. 67
Nini, A. xiii, 36

Olohan, M. 48
orthophemism 13–14
Orwell, George xiv, 58, 60–61, 65, **66**; *see also Animal Farm* (Orwell)
Othello (Shakespeare) 56

Pagano, A. S. xiv
paraphrasing: as communication strategy 10, **11**, 14–15, 17; free paraphrases 111–112, **112**; medical terms and 15, 17–18; microcontexts and 114–115; multiword terms (MWTs) and 105, 109, 111–112, 114–115; prepositional 109; semantic relations and 109, 115; sensitive bodily functions and 15; sexual health communication 13–14, 17; verb paraphrases 109, 111, **111**, 112, *112*, 114–115
Persian health communication: BabelDr machine translation system 2, 8–10; communication strategies (CSs) 3, 7–11, **11**, 12–16, **16**, 17, 19; deletion and 13; euphemisms and 7–11, **11**, 12, 17–18; formal word use 13–14, 17–18; implication and 12–13; metonymy and 15, 17; paraphrasing 14–15, 17; sensitive concepts 2–3, 8–11, 15–18; taboo-related diseases and 7–8, 11; transliteration and 11–12
phraselators: consolidating 17–18; doctor development of 2–3, 18; doctor/nonmedical comparison 16–17, 19; medical communication and 2; sexual health communication 16–17; sexual health variants 10
Pitt, M. B. 14
Plenary, The 44
Polotsk, I. 61, 63, 65, **66**, 72–74, 76
post-editing: cognitive aspects of 85; conceptual text complexity and 83–84, 96–97, **98**, 100–101; co-reference pronouns 97, **97**; effort and 83–85, 90, 94, 100–101; evaluation system 91,

91; free mode data collection 89, *89*; guided mode data collection system 89, *90*; linear regression output 94, **95**, 100–101; machine translation quality and 84, 94, 99, **99**; quality and 83–86, 90–93, *93*, 94–97, 100–101; semantic annotations and 84, 91–92, **92**, 93, 95–96, **98**, 100–101; source data 86–88; technical aspects of 85; temporal effort 85
Pribylovskij, V. 61, 63, 65, **66**, 73–74, 76–77
PropBank inventory 109
Purcell, E. 28

RDF *see* Resource Description Framework (RDF)
Resource Description Framework (RDF) 86, **86**, 87
retranslations: canonical forms and 56; corpus methods for 57–65, 67–68, 70–78; distance measures 58–59, 68, **69**, 70, *70*, 71; domesticated 57, 65, 68, 77; keyword analysis 59–60, 71–73, 75–77; reasons for 56–57; stages of 57; *see also Animal Farm* (Orwell)
Role and Reference Grammar 113
Rosario, B. 107–109
Russian National Corpus 74

Sánchez Ramos, M.del Mar xiii
Schulz, M. 46
semantic annotations: Comics Character category 94–95, *95*, 96, 101; Food category 95–96, **96**, 101; machine translations and xiv, 92; post-edited translations and 84, 91–92, **92**, 93; post-editing quality and 93, 95–96, **98**, 100–101; text complexity and 83–84, 87, 93–94; verbalization and 98, **98**
semantics: categories 105–111, **112**, 113, 115–116, **116**, 117–118; conceptual text complexity and 83, 100–101; multiword terms (MWTs) and 107–111; paraphrasing and 109, 115; patterns 107–108; relations 109–115, 117; roles 105, 107–110, 113
Serrant-Green, L. 15

sexual health communication: communication strategies (CSs) and 16–17; deletion and 13; education and 8; euphemisms and 2, 7, 10–12, **16**, 17; formal word use 13–14, **16**, 17; implication and 12–13; paraphrasing 14–15, 17; as taboo subject 4–5, 18; transliteration and 12
Shakespeare, William 56–57
Sketch Engine 59–60, 110
speech translation systems 2
Štajner, S. 83
Stewart, M. 15, 18
Struve, G. 61, 63–65, **66**, 71–72, **72**, 73–74, 76

Taber, C. 67
taboo language: euphemisms and 4–5, 7, 11; medical communication and 4, 7–8, 10; Persian speakers and 5, 7–8, 10–11
Task, S. 61, 63, 65, **66**, 67, 70, 72–77
Termium Plus 119
TextHammer 61, 78n1
THAT types 48, 50–51
Thucydides 58
translations: aligning multiple 78; channel and 34; conceptual variation in 114; keyword analysis 60; length of 67; microcontexts and 118–119; participant relations and 34; scene in 33–34; situation in 33–34; social evaluation in 34; term variants in 113–114; THAT in 48; *see also* human translations; machine translations; post-editing; retranslations
translation studies (TS): corpus-based 26, 78; empirical xiii, 28; MDA and 27–28, 32–34, 51–52; multivariate approaches in 32–33; retranslations and 57, 78
translation universals 26
translator style 26
transliteration 10–11, **11**, 12, 16
Traumer, L. 15

Universitat Jaume I (Castellón, Spain) 34

Van Rooy, B. 32–33
van Wieringen, J. C. 3

Veirano-Pinto, M. 32
verbalization 96, 98, **98**
Verb-Net 113
Vieira, L. N. 83

Warren, B. 6, 10–13, 15
WebNLG 84, 86–87, *87*, 88, 92

Weijts, W. 12–13, 15
White, P. R. R. 34
WordFast 61
WordSmith Tools xiv, 57, 59
World Wide Web Consortium (W3C) 86

Xiao, R. 30, 32